# Pious Fraud:

## How Religion Has Evolved Throughout History

# Pious Fraud:

## How Religion Has Evolved Throughout History

Irene McGarvie

Based in part on
*"Astral Worship"*
by J.H. Hill

Ancient Wisdom Publishing
a division of Nixon-Carre Ltd., Toronto, ON

## Library and Archives Canada Cataloguing in Publication

McGarvie, Irene, 1957-
    Pious Fraud: How religion has evolved throughout history / Irene McGarvie.

Includes index.
ISBN 978-1-926826-02-8

    1. Religion--History.  2. Natural theology.  I. Title.

BL430.M35 2010            210                    C2010-903166-0




## Published by:  Ancient Wisdom Publishing
(A division of Nixon-Carre Ltd.)
P.O. Box 92533 Carlton RPO
Toronto, Ontario, M5A 4N9

www.learnancientwisdom.com
www.nixon-carre.com

Distributed by Ingram 1-800-937-8000
www.ingrambook.com

Cover image: www.istockphoto.com

**Disclaimer:**
This publication is sold with the understanding that the publishers are not engaged in rendering legal, medical or other professional advice. The information contained herein represents the experiences and opinions of the author, but the author or the publisher are not responsible for the results of any action taken on the basis of information in this work, nor for any errors or omissions.

**Printed and bound in the USA**

# Contents

v

# Introduction

There is nothing new in this book. I do not claim to have created or discovered any of the information compiled here. While much of this book is taken from the classic book *"Astral Worship"* by J.H. Hill, the information has been in front of us for centuries, in numerous forms from varied sources. This is not a scholarly tome. I have attempted to make it clear and easy to understand in order to make this information available to the widest group of readers possible.

Like most people in our society, I grew up exposed to all of the Sunday school stories; Adam and Eve, Jonah and the whale, Noah and the ark, and Jesus' birth in a manger in Bethlehem. I was told that these were historical events and I believed what I was told. Early in my adult life I was exposed to Evangelical Christianity and I believed what I was told, and even taught these same stories to my children.

Sure, in reading the Bible I noticed certain inconsistencies, but it was easy for me to blame it on problems of translation or cultural misunderstandings. Besides, I was told to just believe and have faith.

It was not until I began to learn about other world religions, in particular the earlier pagan teachings, that I realized that the Bible was not a history book but rather a collection of allegorical stories compiled from earlier religious traditions. There were many examples of stories that were too similar to earlier stories for it to be a coincidence. This changed my entire perception of religion in general, and Christianity in particular.

I hope that you will read this book with an open mind. I think that as you read you will be as amazed as I was to realize how obvious it is that we have all been victims of a Pious Fraud.

Irene McGarvie
May 7, 2010

# How It All Began

**1**

## Universal questions

Since the beginning of time human beings have sought answers to the universal questions "What is the purpose of life?", "Why am I here?", and "What happens after death?" Religion developed as man's attempt to answer these universal questions.

In this book I will show how all of our present day religious beliefs, and Christianity in particular, came from one early form of religion. How religious leaders throughout history have adapted these religious beliefs in an attempt to control their followers.

Generally, all of our western religions are based on the premise that God, the creator and boss of the universe (the man in the sky), spoke directly to some prophet explaining the mysteries of life and giving him (the prophets were usually men) the rules that we mortals must live by. Each religion believes that their founder got these rules directly from God and that while other religions may have gotten some of it right, theirs is the only true and complete version.

However, as you read through this book you will be amazed to discover that the literal "truths" and "historical events" that are espoused by our present day Christian churches, and have formed much of our present day religious beliefs, were actually based on much earlier pagan myths.

So, let's step back in history and look at how these beliefs got started.

## A geocentric universe

The founders of the early belief system that forms the basis of our present day religions were a sect of philosophers, known as magi or wise men, from central Asia. Through their contemplation and study of nature they formulated the belief that everything in the universe is animated by a great soul or spirit.

These ancient magi were the astronomers of their day. They observed the movement of the stars, the planets and the patterns in the sky, and concluded that the universe was earth centered, or geocentric. One of the first "truths" that they observed was that the sun, the moon and the planets all rotated around the earth.

## Astrolatry or Sabaism

The earliest religion, what we commonly refer to as paganism, was the worship of nature. Humans observed the seasons, and the cycles of nature, and realized how dependent we are on the energy of the sun. Although they paid homage to all the elements, special respect was reserved for the divinity believed to reside in the sun. Worship of the sun or other heavenly bodies is referred to as Astrolatry or Sabaism.

## Astronomical allegories

An allegory is a story, a fable, which has a deeper meaning than what appears on the surface. Allegories are used in an attempt to explain an abstract or spiritual concept in a more concrete manner, a way of making difficult to understand concepts easier to grasp. The ancient wise men created a religion based on allegorical astronomy. They personified the objects of worship. In other words, they created stories about man-like gods to explain the forces of nature in a manner that the common man could more easily understand.

Unfortunately, to give these stories an air of credibility they claimed to have composed them under the inspiration of the gods. They called these allegorical stories sacred records, or scriptures, and taught the ignorant masses that they were literal histories, about real people, who, having once lived upon earth, and for the good of mankind, performed the wondrous works imputed to them, and were now back in heaven from whence they came.

## Heaven and Hell

Originally, none of the early pagan religions taught anything about a future life. The original belief was that immediately after death the soul was absorbed back into the energy source of nature where all personal identity was forever lost, similar to water flowing from a stream into a river where it merges with the other water and is no longer distinguishable.

## The Sadducees

At the beginning of the Christian era there were still

in existence a sect of Jews known as Sadducees, who were strict adherents to a primitive form of worship. Their belief regarding the state of the dead is recorded in Ecclesiastes 12:7, which reads: *"Then shall the dust return to earth as it was, and the spirit shall return to God who gave it."*

An example of this form of religion was ancient Judaism as portrayed in the Old Testament, more especially in the Pentateuch, or first five books of the Old Testament. You will notice that in the 28th chapter of Deuteronomy, which is a general summing up of the blessings and curses to be enjoyed or suffered for the observance or violation of God's laws, there is no mention of heaven or hell. All the rewards are of an earthly nature.

## Deuteronomy 28 (King James Version)

I have included the entire chapter here because I think it is important for understanding the purpose of religion, which is to control the population.

It takes 68 verses to say basically obey the rules and you will receive blessings during your life, disobey the rules and you will have trouble. It is the carrot and the stick. Behave and you will get a treat, violate the rules and you will be punished. **But nowhere in this chapter is there any mention of a life after death.**

> *1 And it shall come to pass, if thou shalt hearken diligently unto the voice of the LORD thy God, to observe and to do all his commandments which I command thee this day, that the LORD thy God will set thee on high above all nations of the earth:*

*2 And all these blessings shall come on thee, and overtake thee, if thou shalt hearken unto the voice of the LORD thy God.*

*3 Blessed shalt thou be in the city, and blessed shalt thou be in the field.*

*4 Blessed shall be the fruit of thy body, and the fruit of thy ground, and the fruit of thy cattle, the increase of thy kine, and the flocks of thy sheep.*

*5 Blessed shall be thy basket and thy store.*

*6 Blessed shalt thou be when thou comest in, and blessed shalt thou be when thou goest out.*

*7 The LORD shall cause thine enemies that rise up against thee to be smitten before thy face: they shall come out against thee one way, and flee before thee seven ways.*

*8 The LORD shall command the blessing upon thee in thy storehouses, and in all that thou settest thine hand unto; and he shall bless thee in the land which the LORD thy God giveth thee.*

*9 The LORD shall establish thee an holy people unto himself, as he hath sworn unto thee, if thou shalt keep the commandments of the LORD thy God, and walk in his ways.*

*10 And all people of the earth shall see that thou art called by the name of the LORD; and they shall be afraid of thee.*

*11 And the LORD shall make thee plenteous in goods, in the fruit of thy body, and in the fruit of thy cattle, and in the fruit of thy ground, in the land which the LORD sware unto thy fathers to give thee.*

*12 The LORD shall open unto thee his good treasure, the heaven to give the rain unto thy land in his season, and to bless all the work of thine hand: and thou shalt lend unto many nations, and thou shalt not borrow.*

*13 And the LORD shall make thee the head, and not the tail; and thou shalt be above only, and thou shalt not be beneath; if that thou hearken unto the commandments of the LORD thy God, which I command thee this day, to observe and to do them:*

*14 And thou shalt not go aside from any of the words which I command thee this day, to the right hand, or to the left, to go after other gods to serve them.*

*15 But it shall come to pass, if thou wilt not hearken unto the voice of the LORD thy God, to observe to do all his commandments and his statutes which I command thee this day; that all these curses shall come upon thee, and overtake thee:*

*16 Cursed shalt thou be in the city, and cursed shalt thou be in the field.*

*17 Cursed shall be thy basket and thy store.*

*18 Cursed shall be the fruit of thy body, and the fruit of thy land, the increase of thy kine, and the flocks of thy sheep.*

*19* Cursed shalt thou be when thou comest in, and cursed shalt thou be when thou goest out.

*20* The LORD shall send upon thee cursing, vexation, and rebuke, in all that thou settest thine hand unto for to do, until thou be destroyed, and until thou perish quickly; because of the wickedness of thy doings, whereby thou hast forsaken me.

*21* The LORD shall make the pestilence cleave unto thee, until he have consumed thee from off the land, whither thou goest to possess it.

*22* The LORD shall smite thee with a consumption, and with a fever, and with an inflammation, and with an extreme burning, and with the sword, and with blasting, and with mildew; and they shall pursue thee until thou perish.

*23* And thy heaven that is over thy head shall be brass, and the earth that is under thee shall be iron.

*24* The LORD shall make the rain of thy land powder and dust: from heaven shall it come down upon thee, until thou be destroyed.

*25* The LORD shall cause thee to be smitten before thine enemies: thou shalt go out one way against them, and flee seven ways before them: and shalt be removed into all the kingdoms of the earth.

*26* And thy carcase shall be meat unto all fowls of the air, and unto the beasts of the earth, and no man shall fray them away.

*27 The LORD will smite thee with the botch of Egypt, and with the emerods, and with the scab, and with the itch, whereof thou canst not be healed.*

*28 The LORD shall smite thee with madness, and blindness, and astonishment of heart:*

*29 And thou shalt grope at noonday, as the blind gropeth in darkness, and thou shalt not prosper in thy ways: and thou shalt be only oppressed and spoiled evermore, and no man shall save thee.*

*30 Thou shalt betroth a wife, and another man shall lie with her: thou shalt build an house, and thou shalt not dwell therein: thou shalt plant a vineyard, and shalt not gather the grapes thereof.*

*31 Thine ox shall be slain before thine eyes, and thou shalt not eat thereof: thine ass shall be violently taken away from before thy face, and shall not be restored to thee: thy sheep shall be given unto thine enemies, and thou shalt have none to rescue them.*

*32 Thy sons and thy daughters shall be given unto another people, and thine eyes shall look, and fail with longing for them all the day long; and there shall be no might in thine hand.*

*33 The fruit of thy land, and all thy labours, shall a nation which thou knowest not eat up; and thou shalt be only oppressed and crushed alway:*

*34 So that thou shalt be mad for the sight of thine eyes*

*which thou shalt see.*

**35** *The LORD shall smite thee in the knees, and in the legs, with a sore botch that cannot be healed, from the sole of thy foot unto the top of thy head.*

**36** *The LORD shall bring thee, and thy king which thou shalt set over thee, unto a nation which neither thou nor thy fathers have known; and there shalt thou serve other gods, wood and stone.*

**37** *And thou shalt become an astonishment, a proverb, and a byword, among all nations whither the LORD shall lead thee.*

**38** *Thou shalt carry much seed out into the field, and shalt gather but little in; for the locust shall consume it.*

**39** *Thou shalt plant vineyards, and dress them, but shalt neither drink of the wine, nor gather the grapes; for the worms shall eat them.*

**40** *Thou shalt have olive trees throughout all thy coasts, but thou shalt not anoint thyself with the oil; for thine olive shall cast his fruit.*

**41** *Thou shalt beget sons and daughters, but thou shalt not enjoy them; for they shall go into captivity.*

**42** *All thy trees and fruit of thy land shall the locust consume.*

**43** *The stranger that is within thee shall get up above thee very high; and thou shalt come down very low.*

**44** *He shall lend to thee, and thou shalt not lend to him: he shall be the head, and thou shalt be the tail.*

**45** *Moreover all these curses shall come upon thee, and shall pursue thee, and overtake thee, till thou be destroyed; because thou hearkenedst not unto the voice of the LORD thy God, to keep his commandments and his statutes which he commanded thee:*

**46** *And they shall be upon thee for a sign and for a wonder, and upon thy seed for ever.*

**47** *Because thou servedst not the LORD thy God with joyfulness, and with gladness of heart, for the abundance of all things;*

**48** *Therefore shalt thou serve thine enemies which the LORD shall send against thee, in hunger, and in thirst, and in nakedness, and in want of all things: and he shall put a yoke of iron upon thy neck, until he have destroyed thee.*

**49** *The LORD shall bring a nation against thee from far, from the end of the earth, as swift as the eagle flieth; a nation whose tongue thou shalt not understand;*

**50** *A nation of fierce countenance, which shall not regard the person of the old, nor shew favour to the young:*

**51** *And he shall eat the fruit of thy cattle, and the fruit of thy land, until thou be destroyed: which also shall not leave thee either corn, wine, or oil, or the increase of thy* *kine, or flocks of thy sheep, until he hath destroyed thee.*

**52** *And he shall besiege thee in all thy gates, until thy high and fenced walls come down, wherein thou trustedst, throughout all thy land: and he shall besiege thee in all thy gates throughout all thy land, which the LORD thy God hath given thee.*

**53** *And thou shalt eat the fruit of thine own body, the flesh of thy sons and of thy daughters, which the LORD thy God hath given thee, in the siege, and in the straitness, wherewith thine enemies shall distress thee:*

**54** *So that the man that is tender among you, and very delicate, his eye shall be evil toward his brother, and toward the wife of his bosom, and toward the remnant of his children which he shall leave:*

**55** *So that he will not give to any of them of the flesh of his children whom he shall eat: because he hath nothing left him in the siege, and in the straitness, wherewith thine enemies shall distress thee in all thy gates.*

**56** *The tender and delicate woman among you, which would not adventure to set the sole of her foot upon the ground for delicateness and tenderness, her eye shall be evil toward the husband of her bosom, and toward her son, and toward her daughter,*

**57** *And toward her young one that cometh out from between her feet, and toward her children which she shall bear: for she shall eat them for want of all things secretly in the siege and straitness, wherewith thine enemy shall distress thee in thy gates.*

**58** *If thou wilt not observe to do all the words of this law that are written in this book, that thou mayest fear this glorious and fearful name, THE LORD THY GOD;*

**59** *Then the LORD will make thy plagues wonderful, and the plagues of thy seed, even great plagues, and of long continuance, and sore sicknesses, and of long continuance.*

**60** *Moreover he will bring upon thee all the diseases of Egypt, which thou wast afraid of; and they shall cleave unto thee.*

**61** *Also every sickness, and every plague, which is not written in the book of this law, them will the LORD bring upon thee, until thou be destroyed.*

**62** *And ye shall be left few in number, whereas ye were as the stars of heaven for multitude; because thou wouldest not obey the voice of the LORD thy God.*

**63** *And it shall come to pass, that as the LORD rejoiced over you to do you good, and to multiply you; so the LORD will rejoice over you to destroy you, and to bring you to nought; and ye shall be plucked from off the land whither thou goest to possess it.*

**64** *And the LORD shall scatter thee among all people, from the one end of the earth even unto the other; and there thou shalt serve other gods, which neither thou nor hy fathers have known, even wood and stone.*

**65** *And among these nations shalt thou find no ease, neither shall the sole of thy foot have rest: but the LORD* *shall give thee there a trembling heart, and failing of eyes, and sorrow of mind:*

**66** *And thy life shall hang in doubt before thee; and thou shalt fear day and night, and shalt have none assurance of thy life:*

**67** *In the morning thou shalt say, Would God it were even! and at even thou shalt say, Would God it were morning! for the fear of thine heart wherewith thou shalt fear, and for the sight of thine eyes which thou shalt see.*

**68** *And the LORD shall bring thee into Egypt again with ships, by the way whereof I spake unto thee, Thou shalt see it no more again: and there ye shall be sold unto your enemies for bondmen and bondwomen, and no man shall buy you.*

Reading this it is apparent that these laws were intended for the regulation of the society, and to keep the peace among neighbors. In order to ensure their obedience, they were entered into the sacred records and made part of the religion.

## Bad things happen to good people

However, this presented a problem. It is apparent to any casual observer that bad things happen to good people, regardless of how well they obey God's rules, and truly evil people often appear to be successful. It became obvious to those in power that the temporal punishments of these existing laws were not enough of a deterrent to prevent crime, and so it was determined that the ignorant masses could be better governed by appealing to the sentiments of hope and fear in relation to the rewards and punishments of an unseen future life. So the ancient astrologers revised this element of the religion and included the concept of rewards in a future life.

## Philosophy vs. religion

As is so often the case, fixing one problem created another problem. It became necessary to suppress the belief in the absorption of all souls back into the energy source of nature. So, they stopped teaching it to the masses, but continued to teach it to the initiates or elite in the secret system known as the Esoteric philosophy. (Esoteric means intended for, or understood by, only an initiated few.)

They made the change adding the doctrine of future rewards and punishments to the written and openly taught system of faith known as the Exoteric creed. (Exoteric means something that is capable of being understood by most people, not just an informed or select minority.) As a result they created a 2-tiered religion that exists to this day; one for those select few deemed capable of understanding it, and one for the ignorant majority.

Thus the followers of this ancient Astral worship were divided into two distinct classes, the Esoterics, or Gnostics; and the Exoterics. The former comprising those who knew that the Gods were mythical and the scriptures allegorical; and the latter who were taught that the gods were real, and the scriptures historical.

It was a philosophy for the cultured few and a religion for the ignorant multitude. The initiates into the secrets of these two systems recognized them as two gospels. Paul appears to have made reference to this in his Epistle to the Galatians 2:2, where he distinguishes the gospel which he preached on ordinary occasions from that gospel which he preached *"privately to them which were of reputation."*

This was the system of Astrolatry, which became the state religion of the Grecian and Roman Empires and which culminated in the fourth century in the substitution of Christianity as the state religion of the Roman Empire. As you continue to read through this book you will see how the changes made during the sixth century resulted in the creation of the Muslim faith, and how changes in the Middle Ages and during the Reformation of the sixteenth century, evolved into Catholicism and Protestantism.

You will also see how Freemasonry and Druidism were simply different forms of this ancient religion/philosophy of Astrolatry.

## Rev. Robert Taylor "The Devil's Chaplain"

While much of this book is based on the classic book *"Astral Worship"* by J. H. Hill, I am also indebted to the research of Reverend Robert Taylor (1784-1844) dubbed "the Devil's Chaplain."

Taylor was an Anglican clergyman who left the church and turned "Freethinker" when his research into early Christianity convinced him that the traditional story of Christian origins as taught by all Christian churches was not only inaccurate, but was deliberately designed to manipulate and control the masses.

Taylor's book, "*The Diegesis*" was written in England in 1828, while he was in prison for one year having been convicted of blasphemy and conspiracy to overthrow the Christian religion. He was again sentenced to two years in prison for blasphemy in April 1831. Taylor's imprisonment served as a warning to others not to attempt to stand up to the religious establishment.

# The Geocentric System of Nature

*2*

Understanding a bit about the ancient scientific beliefs about the universe helps us to understand how our present day religious beliefs developed.

## The Earth as the center of the universe

The ancients believed that the earth was the only world, that it was a vast flat circular plane, the fixed and immovable center around which all other celestial bodies revolved. The universe was "geocentric" or "earth centered".

Eventually, astrologers came to the realization that the earth was not flat but spherical, and that the universe revolved around the sun, was "heliocentric." Archeological research has suggested that astronomers invented the telescope and discovered the true or heliocentric system of nature several centuries before the beginning of the Christian era. But because the religion had been based upon the geocentric system, it was deemed prudent not to teach it to the masses.

Some of the earliest astrologers to question the geocentric theory included Philolaus (c. 480-385 BCE), who described an astronomical system in which the Earth, Moon, Sun, planets, and stars all revolved about a central fire; Heraclides Ponticus (387-312 BCE) who proposed that the Earth rotates on its axis; and Aristarchus of Samos (310-230 BCE) who developed the heliocentric hypotheses that the earth revolved around the sun.

However, since these theories contradicted the official doctrine of the church, they were condemned as false and contrary to scripture, and were hidden away among the other secrets of the esoteric philosophy, and the knowledge of it was lost. When it was rediscovered, the hierarchy of the Church of Rome resorted to inquisitorial tortures to suppress it.

Nicolaus Copernicus (1473 -1543) published a book, *"On the Revolutions of the Celestial Spheres,"* in 1543, just prior to his death, which outlined his hypothesis that the earth revolved around the sun.

In 1632 Galileo Galilei wrote his most famous work titled *"Dialogue Concerning the Two Chief World Systems,"* where he expanded on Copernicus' earlier work and explained the actual nature of the universe. As a result he was tried by the Inquisition, found guilty of heresy, was forced to recant his research, and spent the rest of his life under house arrest as a warning to others who might be tempted to make this information widely known.

## The nether world

Once the doctrine of future rewards and punishments was developed, it was believed that the world was divided into an upper and lower (nether) world, which was connected by a sinuous and dark shadowy passage.

## The firmament

The azure blue dome above the earth, what we refer to as the sky, is called the firmament in the creation story in Genesis 1:6-8, and was believed to be a solid transparency.

> God said, "Let there be a firmament in the midst of the waters, and let it divide the waters from the waters. And God made the firmament, and divided the waters which were under the firmament from the waters which were above the firmament: and it was so. And God called the firmament Heaven. And the evening and the morning were the second day."

Genesis 1:20, explains that the firmament is above the Earth:

> Then God said, "Let the waters abound with an abundance of living creatures, and let the birds fly above the earth across the face of the firmament of the heavens".

The sky or firmament is described as a strong crystalline material in Job 37:18:

> "Hast thou with him spread out the sky, which is strong, and as a molten looking glass?"

This firmament is described in Revelation 4:6 *"as a sea of glass like unto crystal."* It was characterized as being supported by four pillars, resting upon the earth, one at each of the cardinal points, north, south, east, and west, which were designated as *"the pillars of heaven."*

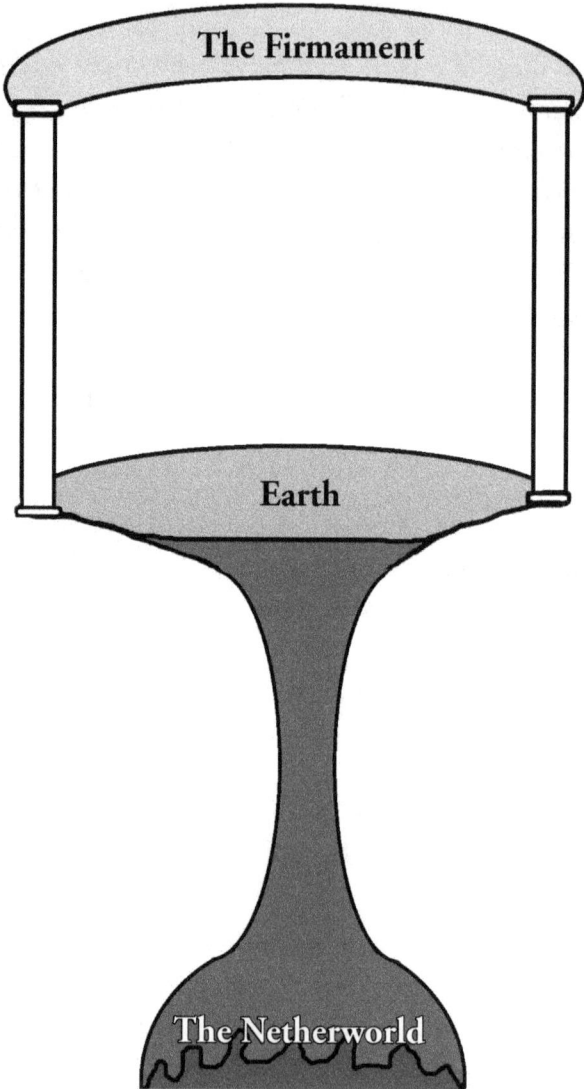

These pillars of heaven are mentioned in Job 26:11:

*"The pillars of heaven tremble and are astonished at his reproof."*

Conceiving the idea that there were windows in the firmament, the ancient astronomers called them *"the windows of heaven"* and taught that they were opened when it rained, and closed when it ceased to rain. There is a reference to this in Genesis 7:11 (KJV):

*"In the six hundredth year of Noah's life, in the second month, the seventeenth day of the month, the same day were all the fountains of the great deep broken up, and the windows of heaven were opened.*

In Genesis 8:2 (KJV):

*"The fountains also of the deep and the windows of heaven were stopped, and the rain from heaven was restrained."*

Heaven is above the firmament according to the Genesis story about the Tower of Babel, the construction of a tall tower to reach to the heavens in Genesis 11:4.

*"And they said, Go to, let us build us a city and a tower, whose top may reach unto heaven."*

## The stars

The ancients believed that the stars were candles or torches suspended from the firmament, and which revolved around the earth to give it light and heat.

# The planets

The ancient astronomers observed that seven of these lights, the Sun, Moon, Mercury, Venus, Mars, Jupiter and Saturn, had perceptible movements in relation to the other lights in the sky, so they referred to them as planets or wandering stars.

## The constellations

Noticing that the other celestial lights maintained the same relation to each other, and designating them as fixed stars, the ancient astronomers grouped those visible to them into forty-eight constellations; and gave them names. They also attached names to the largest of the stars in order to locate and distinguish them more easily.

## The Zodiac

Through twelve of these constellations (mostly contained within a belt of 16 degrees in width, and within which the planets appeared to revolve), the ancient astronomers drew a central line representing the apparent orbit of the sun. They divided this central line into 360 degrees; each quarter representing one of the seasons. They named the 4 cardinal points the summer and winter solstices, and the vernal and autumnal equinoxes; the former referring to the longest and shortest days of the year; and the latter to the two times when the days and nights are equal.

A series of symbols representing each of these constellations became known as the zodiac, or *"circle of living creatures"* which is referred to in Ezekial chapter 1.

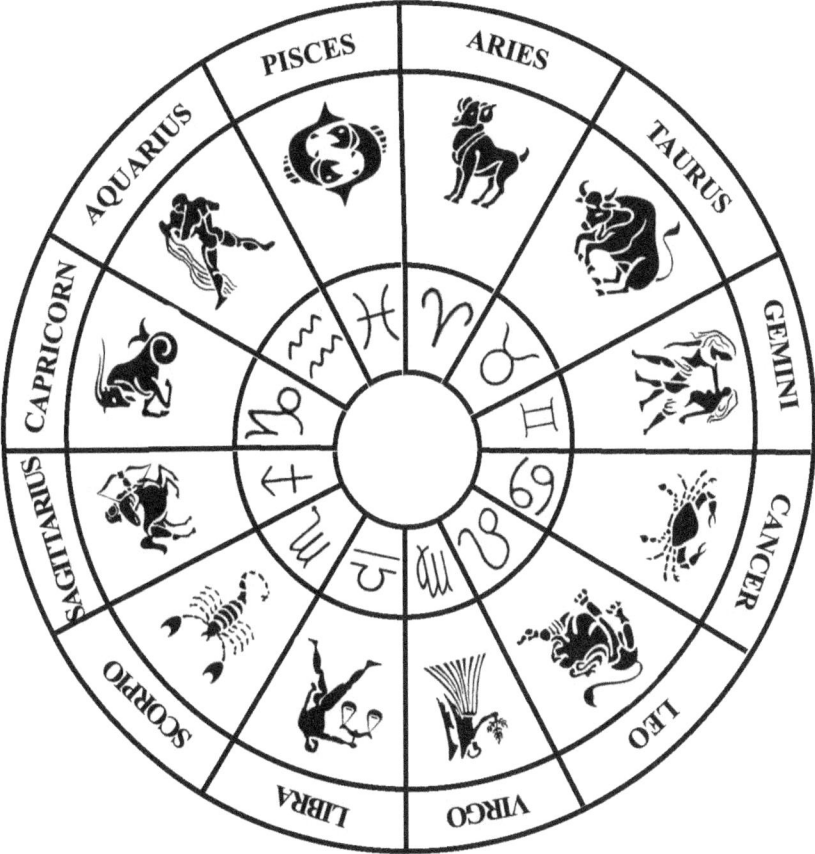

*"I do not feel obliged to believe
that the same God who has endowed us with
sense, reason, and intellect has intended us to
forgo their use."*

**Galileo Galilei**

# 3

# Solar Worship and Christianity

In this chapter you will see how the doctrines of Astral or Solar worship form the basis of modern day Christianity.

## The sacred numbers 7 and 12

The numbers seven and twelve were considered sacred by the ancient astrologers, and dedications were made to them in many ways.

In Revelation 4:5, we find one of many references to the number seven:

*"Seven lamps of fire burning before the throne, which are the seven spirits of God."*

Seven branched candlesticks were laid down in front of the altars in ancient temples; the central light for the Sun; the Moon, Mercury and Venus on one side; and Mars, Jupiter and Saturn on the other. The seven branched candlesticks seen in all Catholic churches, and in some Protestant ones, represent the same planetary system.

In the allegories (religious myths), the genii (guardian spirits or gods) of the planets were messengers to the Supreme Deity, the man in the sky who was enthroned above the firmament.

Among the numerous dedications to the genii of the planets are the seven days of the week, the seven stories of the tower of Babylon, the seven gates of Thebes, the seven piped flute of Pan, the seven stringed lyre of Apollo, the seven books of fate, the book of seven seals, the seven castes into which the Egyptians and Hindus were divided, and the jubilee of seven times seven years.

Among the dedications to the twelve signs are the twelve months of the year, the grand cycle of 12,000 years, the twelve altars of James, the twelve labors of Hercules, the twelve divisions of the Egyptian Labyrinth, the twelve shields of Mars, the twelve precious stones (ranged in threes to denote the seasons) in the breastplate of the High Priest, the twelve foundations of the Sacred City referred to in the Book of Revelation, the twelve sons of Jacob, the twelve tribes of Israel, and the twelve Disciples. In the Book of Revelation alone, the number 7 is repeated twenty-four times and the number 12 fourteen times.

## The 12,000 year cycle

The ancient astrologers dedicated a thousand years to each of the signs of the zodiac, thus initiating a cycle of twelve thousand years. They taught that at the conclusion of the cycle, the heaven and the earth which they believed to be composed of the indestructible elements of fire, air, earth and water, would through fire, be reduced to chaos. This would result in the creation of a new heaven and a new earth at the beginning of the succeeding cycle.

## The ancient triad

After conceiving the idea of a primeval chaos, made up of four indestructible elements of which fire was the leading one, the Oriental astrologers began to speculate about what caused the cycle to begin. They attributed this work to three intelligences which they personified by the figure of a man with three heads, and called them Brahma, Vishnu and Siva. Such a figure is believed to represent the Creator, Preserver and Destroyer, one power which had 3 names, 3 characteristics.

The first person represents neither the creator nor organizer of chaos, but chaos itself. The second is its organizer and governor. The third provides life and motion, the great soul or spirit in the esoteric philosophy. The Egyptian triad of Father, Son and Spirit is virtually the same one as the original Oriental philosophy. Therefore, we see that the Christian concept of the trinity comes from ancient Astrolatry.

"God the Father, God the Son,
God the Spirit -- three in one."

The ancient triad consisted of the Father, the Word and the Holy Ghost, which we find recorded in 1 John 5:7, which reads that:

*"There are three that bear record in heaven, the Father, the Word and the Holy Ghost, and these three are one."*

In some forms of Astrolatry it was considered too

sacred to attach a name to the three-part deity, so he was called "the One". We find an example of this in the 4th chapter of Revelation, where, like Zeus and Jupiter of the Grecian and Roman mythologies, he is represented as seated above the firmament upon a throne from which lightning and thunder erupted, and to whom all the subordinate divinities were made to serve. As the hurler of thunderbolts he was called "the Thunderer," and as the opener of the windows of heaven when it rained, he was designated "Jupiter Pluvius".

There is an ancient inscription found in the ruins of the temple at Sais in Egypt:

*"I am all that has been, all that is, and all that shall be, and no mortal has lifted yet the veil that covers me."*

Pliny, the Roman philosopher and naturalist, wrote this about the concept of God in the first century of the Christian era:

*"An infinite God which has never been created, and which shall never come to an end. To look for something else beyond it is useless labor for man and out of his reach. Behold that truly sacred Being, eternal and immense, which includes within itself everything; it is All in All, or rather itself is All. It is the work of nature, and itself is nature."*

We see that although the myths honored a multitude of subordinate divinities, ancient Astrolatry, like Hinduism today, was only an apparent polytheism; its more enlightened devotees, recognizing the dogma of the unity of God, were in reality monotheists, honoring the mythical god of the sun.

## God Sol or Sun God

To understand the characteristics of the supreme divinity of astral worship, you must remember that its founders taught that he was created by the Father, or first person in the sacred triad, from his pure substance. This substance consisted of chaos or the primeval fire in which they believed all things were consumed at the conclusion of each 12,000 year cycle.

Hence, designating that mythical being as the only begotten of the Father, they personified him as God the Son, or second person in the sacred triad; and recognizing the sun as the ruling star, very appropriately made him the presiding god of the sun, under the title of "God Sol". He is referred to in the allegories (the scriptures) as *"The true Light, which lighteth every man that cometh into the world,"* John 1:9, and although designated as the only begotten of the Father, his co-existence with him, under the title of the "Logos" or "Word", is shown in the text which reads, *"In the beginning was the Word, and the Word was with God, and the Word was God,"* John 1:1.

## Good vs. evil

Personifying the principles of good and evil in God Sol, the ancient astrologers consecrated the reproductive months of spring and summer to him as Lord of Good, and they dedicated the destructive months of autumn and winter, to him as Lord of Evil. Personifying in him the opposing principles of good and evil, he was to the ancients both God and the Devil, or the varied God, who in relation to the seasons was described as beautiful in spring, powerful in summer, in decline in autumn and terrible in winter.

# The Constellations Hercules and Draco

## The Constellation Serpens

Thus under various names intended to represent God Sol in relation to the different seasons, we find recorded in the scriptures, or solar fables, numerous portrayals of imaginary conflicts in which the evil being triumphs during autumn and winter, but is conquered at the vernal equinox by the good being, who brings back equal days and nights and restores the harmony of nature.

The eternal conflict between the principles of good and evil, as manifested in the diversity of the seasons, is portrayed in the constellations Hercules and Draco. The heel of the former, representing one of the most ancient of the imaginary incarnations of God Sol, is resting upon the head of the latter, as referred to in Genesis 3:15, where God says to the serpent, *"I will put enmity between thee and the woman, and between thy seed and her seed; it shall bruise thy head, and thou shalt bruise his heel."* The woman alluded to in this text is the Virgo of the zodiac.

Of all the divinities of the ancient mythology, God Sol was the only one that held the title of Lord or Lord God, because he was the organizer of chaos and governor of heaven and earth. Therefore, having established him as the lord of light and darkness, as well as good and evil, the ancient astrologers in composing the solar fables made him say, *"I form the light and create darkness; I make peace and create evil, I the Lord do all these things,"* Isaiah 45: 7. *"Shall there be evil in a city, and the Lord hath not done it?"* Amos 3:6.

Besides the title of Lord or Lord God, the solar divinity is also designated in the allegories as the Lord of Lords and the King of Kings, the Invincible, the Mighty God, etc.

## The virgin birth

During his annual revolution around the earth, the mythical god of the sun symbolizes the four stages of human life from infancy to old age. Therefore, the ancient magi fixed the birth day of the young God Sol at the winter solstice. The Virgo of the zodiac was his mother, and the constellation in conjunction with her, which is now known as Bootes, but anciently called Arcturus, was his foster father. He is depicted  as holding the leashes of two hunting dogs and driving Ursa Major, or the Great Bear, around the north pole. Thus showing that the original job of the celestial foster father of the young God Sol was that of a bear driver, and that his sons, referred to in Job 38: 32, are the dogs Asterion and Chara. Virgo is represented with a child in her arms. It was taught that she was the only virgin who could give birth to a child and be a virgin still.

# The Constellation Virgo

## The ancient cosmogony

Speculating about how chaos had been organized, the ancient astrologers constructed a cosmogony (theory of the origin of the universe), which divided the labors of God the Son, or second person in the trinity, into six periods. They taught that in the first period he made the earth; in the second, the firmament; in the third, vegetation; in the fourth, the sun and moon and "the stars also;" in the fifth, the animals, fishes, birds, etc., and in the sixth, man.

That vegetation was made before the sun was not an inconsistent idea to the originators of the ancient cosmogony. They imagined that the heat and light, emanating from the elementary fire, were sufficient to stimulate its growth, after which God the Son gathered it together and made the celestial bodies. In the solar fables this imaginary element is called the fire-ether, or sacred fire of the stars.

## The fall and redemption of man

Religion having been based upon the worship of personified nature, it appears that its founders developed their religious beliefs from their conceptions of nature's destructive and reproductive processes as manifested in the rotation and diversity of the seasons. The apparent retreat of the sun from the earth, in winter, and its return in the spring, suggesting the idea of a symbolic death and resurrection of the god of the sun, they applied these phenomena of the year to man, and composed the allegories regarding his fall and redemption, as taught in the exoteric creed.

In the allegory relating to the fall, it was taught that, after making the first human pair, the Lord of Good or the Lord God placed them in a beautiful garden - corresponding to the seasons of fruits and flowers or months of spring and summer, with the order not to eat of the fruit of a certain tree. When the Lord of Evil, or the Devil, symbolized by the serpent and represented by the constellation "Serpens" placed in conjunction with the autumnal equinox, tempted the woman, and then she the man, they ate of the forbidden fruit thereby committing the original sin, they involved the whole human race in the consequences of their disobedience. Then the Lord God, pronouncing a curse against the serpent, clothed the man and woman with skins to protect them against the inclement weather and drove them from the garden, after which they needed to earn their bread by tilling the ground.

## A savior every 600 years

The ancient astrologers divided the 6,000 years they appropriated to man, as the duration of his race on earth, into ten equal cycles, and taught that at the conclusion of each cycle (600 years) God Sol, as Lord of Good, would manifest himself in the flesh, to destroy his works as Lord of Evil, and through suffering and death make an atonement for sin. Having originated the doctrines of original sin, incarnation and vicarious atonement, as parts of the plan of redemption, and making its finale correspond, in point of time, to the conclusion of the 12,000 year cycle, they then added the additional religious beliefs regarding the general judgment and future rewards and punishments.

Having based the fables of the fall and redemption of man on the idea that man was forced, without his choice, to pass from the dominion of God to that of the Devil, in the same way that the inclement seasons of autumn and winter succeed the beneficent ones of spring and summer, its authors composed the original of the text which, found in Romans 8:20, reads that *"The creature was made subject to vanity (Evil), not willingly, but by reason of him who hath subjected the same in hope."*

If it were not for the popular teaching of its being actual literal history, no one could read the account of the fall of man, as recorded in the third chapter of Genesis, without recognizing it as simply an allegory; or fail to realize the force of the argument of no fall, no redemption, and if no redemption, no God to reward or Devil to punish; no hell to suffer, or heaven to enjoy. These are contrasting ideas which came in together, and must survive or perish together. They cannot be separated without destroying the whole theory.

## Incarnations of God Sol

Believing that God Sol needed to remain at his post to direct the course of the sun, the ancient astrologers came up with the idea of teaching that, attended by a retinue of subordinate genii or gods, God Sol descended to earth through a variety of incarnations at the end of 600 year cycles, to perform the work of man's redemption. Having made Virgo of the zodiac the mother of the solar divinity, they taught in their allegorical astronomy, or scriptures, that his incarnations were born of a virgin. Hence we find that God Sol, usually designated by the title of the Word, *"was made flesh, and dwelt among us."* John 1:14.

Having assigned to the incarnations of God Sol the characteristics of heaven-descending, virgin-born, earth-walking, wonder-working, dying, resuscitated and ascending sons of God, the ancient astrologers gave them the titles of Savior, Redeemer, Avatar, Divine-Helper, Shiloh, Messiah, Christ; and, in reference to his foster-father, that of Son of Man. Teaching that they continued to make intercession for sin, after their ascension to the right hand of the Father, they were also called intercessors, mediators or advocates with the Father. From this teaching came the Egyptian legend of the Phoenix, a bird said to descend from the sun at these intervals, and, after being consumed upon the altar in the Temple of On, or City of the Sun (called Heliopolis by the Greeks), would rise from its ashes and ascend to heaven.

According to the civil laws of Egypt, manhood was not attained until the age of thirty, hence the earthly mission of incarnate saviors began at that age. Since the sun moved through the twelve signs of the zodiac during the period of one year, the earthly mission of the savior was completed during that same time period.

To impress the ignorant masses with the belief that the scriptures were literal histories, and the incarnate saviors real personages, the ancient astrologers caused tombs to be erected in which it was claimed they were buried. Such sepulchres were erected to Hercules at Cadiz, to Apollo at Delphi, and to other saviors at many other places, to which their respective followers were encouraged to perform pilgrimages. In Egypt the pyramids were built, partly for astronomical purposes, and partly as tombs for saviors, claimed to have been kings, who had once ruled over the country. The magnificent structure known as the Church of the Holy Sepulchre, at Jerusalem, is but another one of those tombs of saviors in which no savior was ever entombed.

So we see that it was God Sol, the only begotten of the Father, or second person in the sacred triad, that was worshipped in all forms of the ancient Astrolatry; and that its cultured priests, understanding that the doctrines pertaining to the fall and redemption of man were evolved from the figurative death and resurrection of the solar divinity, recognized the doctrine of incarnation was a priestly invention intended only for the ignorant masses.

## The fable of the twelve labors

The authors of the original solar fables, having lived in an age in which physical prowess was recognized as the highest attribute of humanity, came up with the idea that God Sol, while passing through his apparent orbit, had to fight his way through the animals of the zodiac, and with others in conjunction with them. Designating him as the Mighty Hunter, and calling his exploits the twelve labors, they made the incarnate saviors the heroes of similar ones on earth, which they taught were performed for the good of mankind; and that, after fulfilling their earthly mission, they were returned to heaven through fire.

When these fables were composed the summer solstice was in the sign of Leo, and making the twelve labors begin in it, the first consisted in the killing of a lion, and the second, in rescuing a virgin (Virgo) by the destruction of a Hydra (the constellation in conjunction with her). On one of the Assyrian marbles on exhibition in the British Museum these two labors are represented as having been performed by a savior by the name of Nimroud. In the constellations of Taurus, the bull of the zodiac, and of Orion, originally known as Horns, we have groupings of stars representing the latter as one of the mighty hunters of the ancient Astrolatry, supporting on his left arm the shield of the lion's skin, the trophy of the first labor, and holding a club in his uplifted right hand, is engaged in performing the tenth labor.

The fable of the twelve labors was part of the sacred records or scriptures of the older forms of Astrolatry, one version of which, written with the cuneiform character on twelve tablets of burnt clay, exhumed from the ruins of an Assyrian city, and now on exhibition in the British Museum, is ascribed to Nimroud, the prototype of the Grecian Hercules, and of Nimrod, the Mighty Hunter of the Old Testament.

*"I am an agnostic;*
*I do not pretend to know what*
*many ignorant men are sure of."*

**Clarence Seward Darrow**
1857-1938 American Lawyer
and Civil Libertarian

# 4

# The Anniversaries of Solar Worship

## How did they come up with the day of the Nativity?

As we saw in the previous chapter, in ancient Astral worship it was taught that a savior would come down from God Sol every 600 years. The savior's one year span was timed to correspond to both the stages of human existence from infancy to mature age, and the cycle of the zodiac. Comparing the first day of life to the shortest day of the year, it would naturally be expected that they would have placed the anniversary of the Nativity exactly at the winter solstice; but, having conceived the idea that the sun stood still for the space of three days at each of the cardinal points, and making it represent the figurative death of the god of the sun, they fixed the date for the birth of the savior three days later, or on the 25th of December.

The Gnostic adherents to the ancient solar worship, or those who were familiar with the teachings of the esoteric philosophy (esoteric meaning that which was hidden from the masses), recognized the woman *"clothed with the sun, and the moon under her feet, and upon her head a crown of twelve stars,"* referred to in Revelations 12:1, as the Virgo of the zodiac;

they also believed that she was the true queen of heaven and mother of God; and that the infant, in her arms, and with whom, in their day, she arose on the eastern horizon at midnight on the 24th of December, was the new born savior.

## Epiphany or Twelfth Day

The twelfth day after Christmas, the 6th of January, was observed by the followers of Astrolatry as the anniversary of the Epiphany or Twelfth Day. In the solar fables, it was taught that a star appeared in the heavens on that day to point out the birthplace of the infant savior to the magi or wise men of the East, who came to pay him homage, and to present him with the gifts of gold, frankincense and myrrh, as related in Matthew 2:11.

The reason for presenting these gifts is explained by the fact that of the seven metals dedicated to the gods of the planets, gold was the one consecrated to God Sol; and frankincense and myrrh were the gums burned in his worship.

## Lent

In the ancient solar fables it was taught that the persecutions to which the incarnate saviors were subjected while passing through the dominion of God Sol as Lord of Evil, raged with greatest fury during the forty days preceding the festival of Easter, which began when the days were perceptibly lengthening, was called Lent, or the Lenten season. It was during this season that the followers of the ancient religion were taught to manifest their sympathy for the savior in his imaginary conflict with the Devil by abstaining from all festivities, and by fasting and prayer. As that was the season in which the flocks and herds were poor in flesh, while the seas and rivers abounded with fish in good condition, the ancient priests, making a virtue of necessity, imposed a diet principally of fish, and for that reason placed the constellation Pisces at the point in the zodiac in which the Lenten season began; which, without regard to the day of the week, was always observed on the 15th day of February, the name of that month having been derived from the Februa, or feast of purification and penance in the old Roman calendar.

At the Council of Nicaea it was decided that the Lenten season would begin on the fourth day of the week, and in reference to the ancient custom of the more devout sprinkling ashes upon their heads at the feast of the Februa, it is called Ash Wednesday.

In all years in which Ash Wednesday does not come on the 15th of February, the Lenten season contains a greater or lesser number than the original assignment of forty days.

## Passion Week

The last seven days of Lent is called Passion Week, in reference to the apparent passage of the sun across the celestial equator at the vernal equinox or 21st of March. The ancient astrologers having conceived the idea that the sun stood still for the space of three days at each of the cardinal points, and making it represent the figurative death of the god of that luminary, it was observed as the anniversary of the vernal crucifixion or passion of the incarnate saviors. In commemoration of their imaginary sufferings and death it was the custom to expose in the temples during the last three days of Passion Week figures representing their dead bodies, over which the followers of solar worship, especially the women, cried loudly. It was in reference to one of these images, in the temple at Jerusalem, to which the jealous Jehovah, considering it a great insult in his own house, directs the attention of Ezekiel, the prophet, who, looking, beheld *"Women weeping for Tammuz"* as recorded in Ezekiel 8:14. This divinity was the Phoenician prototype of the Grecian Adonis, to whom the women of Judea preferred to worship.

It was during the last three days of Passion Week that the devotees of solar worship performed their severest penance. Besides fasting and prayer, the more devout flagellated themselves with whips, slashed themselves with knives, and carried heavy crosses up steep inclines. In ultra-Catholic countries the priests, in imitation of the ancient custom, erect in the churches figures representing the dead savior, over which the laity, especially the women, weep and mourn; and the more devout men cut and slash themselves, and each other; and, in imitation of the trek of Jesus with his cross up Calvary's rugged side, bear heavy crosses up steep hills.

## Passion plays

Ancient dramas representing the passion of incarnate saviors, called passion plays, were staged. The most celebrated of these divine tragedies, known as Prometheus Bound, and composed by the Greek poet Aeschylus, was played at Athens 500 years before the beginning of the Christian era. In Aeschylus' version this sin-atoning savior was not chained to a rock, while vultures preyed on him, as he is often portrayed, but was nailed to a tree. The following is a quote from Potter's translation of the play:

*"Lo, streaming from the fatal tree,*
 *His all atoning blood:*
*Is this the infinite? 'Tis he--*
 *Prometheus and a God.*
*Well might the sun in darkness hide,*
 *And veil his glories in,*
*When God the great Prometheus died*
 *For man, the creature's sin."*

The veiling of the sun, as represented in these plays, having reference to the imaginary sympathy expressed by God Sol for the sufferings of his incarnate son, was shown on stage by shading the lights. The monks of the middle ages enacted plays representing the passion of the Christian savior, and in Bavaria, they have kept up this custom, performing the play every tenth year.

## Resurrection and Easter festival

In keeping with the ancient teachings, the incarnate saviors, considered as figuratively dead for the space of three days at the vernal equinox, or 21st of March, were raised to newness of life after the expiration of that time. Therefore, the 25th of March was celebrated as the anniversary of the vernal resurrection.

On the morning of this day it was customary for the priests to say to the mourners assembled in the temples, *"Be of good cheer, sacred band of initiates; your God has risen from the dead, his pains and his sufferings shall be your salvation."* Another form of this admonition, quoted from an ancient poem in reference to the Phoenician Tammuz, reads as follows:

*"Trust ye saints, your God restored,*
*Trust ye in your risen Lord,*
*For the pains which he endured,*
*Your salvation hath procured."*

Then would begin the festivities of Easter, which comes from Eostre, and derived from the Teutonic mythology, was one of the many names given to the goddess of spring. In the observance of this festival the temples were decorated with flowers; the fires upon the pyres, or the fire-altars, were extinguished and rekindled with new fire, or the sacred fire of the stars, which the astrologers taught was brought down from heaven by the winged god Perseus, the constellation which was in conjunction with the vernal equinox; Paschal candles, lit from the new fire, were distributed to the faithful and the Paschal feast, Easter feast, or the feast of the Passover, was eaten in commemoration of the passion of the incarnate saviors, in other words, of the passage of the sun across the celestial equator.

Today, in imitation of the ancient festivities to honor of the return of spring all Catholic churches, and most Protestant ones, are adorned with flowers, the bells ring out, and "Gloria in Excelsis" and other euphoric songs, are sung.

## Annunciation

The anniversary of the nativity having been placed on the 25th of December, it makes sense that the 25th of March was celebrated as the anniversary of the annunciation, and is still observed on that day, and the duty of saluting the Virgin (Virgo) and announcing her conception by the Holy Ghost or third person in the trinity was assigned to the god of spring.

In the Chaldean version of the gospel story the name of Gabriel was given to this personification of the god of spring, and in the Christian version of that story the angel Gabriel is the one who tells the Virgin Mary that she is carrying the child of God. See Luke 1:26-35.

## Ascension

The anniversary of the ascension is celebrated forty days after Easter. In the ancient world it was celebrated on the 4th of May, and it was taught that the incarnate saviors ascended bodily into heaven, in a golden chariot drawn by four horses elaborately adorned with gilded trappings, all glittering like fire in the sunlight.

We read in 2 Kings 2:11, a classic description of the ascension of one of the incarnate saviors of ancient Judaism, in this case the prophet Elijah's ascension to heaven.

*"And it came to pass, as they still went on, and talked, that, behold, there appeared a chariot of fire, and horses of fire, and parted them both asunder; and Elijah went up by a whirlwind into heaven."* KJV

## Assumption

When the summer solstice was in the sign of Cancer, the sun was in that of Virgo in the month of August, and the anniversary of the Assumption was observed on the 15th of that month, and is still observed today. The fact that the anniversary of the Ascension precedes that of the Assumption explains why Jesus says to his mother (Virgo) soon after his resurrection, *"Touch me not: for I am not yet ascended to my Father."* John 20:17.

## The Lord's Supper/Last Summer

In the ancient solar worship the Lord's Supper was observed just before the anniversary of the autumnal crucifixion; and consisting of bread and wine, in reference to the maturing of the crops and making of the wine. It was a season of thankfulness to the Lord (God Sol) as the giver of all good gifts. Being observed only once a year, it was an anniversary; and the fact that Christians partake of these symbols so frequently during the year indicates that the original significance of the Lord's Supper has been lost.

Transubstantiation, or the conversion of the bread and wine into the actual blood and body of Christ, is a doctrine of the Catholic Church which was derived from a ritual of the ancient solar worship.

In the Matthew 26 we have an account of Jesus administering the last supper to his disciples on the eve of the autumnal crucifixion, and in verse 27 it reads that *"he took the cup, and gave thanks, and gave it to them, saying, Drink ye all of it."*

The compilers of the modern version of the Gospel story copied this from the ancient versions of the old story, which, when observed in remembrance of "Our Lord and Savior Bacchus," was called the Bacchanalia, or feast, of Bacchus. At these orgies the participants give thanks for the wine by not only drinking all of one cup, but many more; in fact they kept on drinking until they fell under the table.

## Autumnal crucifixion

The seasons of spring and summer come to an end

at the autumnal equinox, the 22nd of September, so this became the anniversary of the autumnal crucifixion. The vernal resurrection and autumnal crucifixion, representing the alternate triumph of the personified principles of good and evil, as manifested in the diversity of the seasons, is expressed in two religious pictures. In the one, the savior, appealing as a vigorous young man, surrounded by a brilliant halo, representing the rays of the all-conquering sun of spring, is rising triumphantly from the tomb, before which the demon of winter, or Devil, is seen retreating in the background. In the other, the vanquished savior, represented by the figure of a lean and haggard man, with a crown of thorns upon his head, around which appears a faint halo of the sun's declining rays, and above which is placarded the letters I. N. R. I., the initial letters of Latin words, signifying the life to come, or the eternal life, is suspended upon the cross, at the foot of which his mother Mary (Virgo) is represented as kneeling in a mourning attitude, and by her side is seen a serpent and a skull, the emblems of evil and of death.

## Michaelmas

In the calendar of the ancient astral worship, the fourth day after the autumnal equinox was dedicated to the god of autumn. In the Chaldean allegories the name of Michael was given to this personification, and called Michaelmas, or the feast of Michael. In the Catholic calendar this anniversary is placed on the 29th of September, instead of the 26th of that month, while that of St. Matthew, the god of autumn, which should be placed on the 26th of that month, is observed on the 21st.

# The Council of Nicaea

We can see how the anniversaries of the ancient astral worship, became the important days in the Christian calendar. Some modifications were decided at the Council of Nicaea in the year 325. The Bishops assembled at the council to settle various elements of doctrine, one of which was to have the festival of Easter celebrated on a Sunday (which had been made the Sabbath by the edict of Constantine, in the year 321). It was decided that Easter should be observed on the Sunday of the full moon, which comes on or next after the vernal equinox. Hence, converting it into a movable festival, its associated feasts and fast days were also made movable.

*"Nothing can impose better on the people than verbiage; the less they understand, the more they admire."*

**Saint Gregory,** (540-604 CE)
Pope from 590 until his death

# The Divisions of Time

5

Time is a difficult concept to grasp, so the ancient philosophers developed an interesting system to explain time.

## Personifying the divisions of time

The word "personify" means to assign human qualities to an object or abstract notion. Like an allegory, the intention is to simplify an abstract concept.

In the ancient solar fables the divisions of time were personified and made to show reverence to the triune deity, who was thought to be enthroned above the firmament.

## The hours

The guardian spirit/genii/gods of the hours were designated as Elders, and we find them described in Revelation chapter 4 as sitting around the throne on 24 seats, clothed in white and wearing crowns of gold.

# The days

Each day of the year was appropriately personified, and these guardian spirits or genii of the days correspond to the saints of the Christian calendar.

The ancients believed that the sun stood still for three days at each of the four cardinal points, the summer and winter solstices, and the vernal and autumnal equinoxes; the former referring to the longest and shortest days of the year; and the latter to the two periods when the days and nights are equal. The summer solstice, approximately the 24th of June is the first of the decreasing days, and was dedicated to the birth of St. John the Baptist. He is the opposite of Jesus, the guardian spirit of the 25th of December, and first of the increasing days, the winter solstice.

In John 3:30, John the Baptist says *"He must increase, but I must decrease."* If you look at this story from the perspective of astral worship you can see that this simply means that the days of the one must increase in length, while the days of the other must decrease. On December 25th the days begin to get longer, while on June 24th the days get shorter.

# The months

The gods of the twelve signs of the zodiac, corresponding to the months, were called angels and their function was to serve God Sol while he made his annual revolution. However, when they became the attendants of the incarnate saviors during their imaginary earth life, they were personified as men and called disciples.

Of these gods of the months two are particularly interesting for our purposes. The first month, dedicated to the god known in the mythology as Janus, and from which was derived the name January, was portrayed with two faces, the one of an old man looking mournfully backward over the old year, and the other of a young man looking joyfully forward to the new year. This personification, the opener of the year, and represented as holding a pair of cross-keys, was called *"The carrier of the keys of the kingdom of heaven."* Hence, the Popes of Rome, claiming apostolic succession from Peter, the Janus of the Christian twelve, wear cross-keys as the insignia of their office. Sometimes a crosier, or shepherd's crook, is substituted for one of the keys, in reference to his position as the leader of the sheep. The authority for the assumption that the Popes are Peter's successors is found in Matthew 16:18-19, but its meaning changes completely when think of the scriptures as collections of astronomical allegories, and that the Peter referred to in the text was not a man, but the mythical god of the month of January.

In the last month of the year, we find that the authors of the ancient solar fables, doubting whether God Sol, after creating winter by his supposed retreat from the earth, would ever return to revive nature with his life-giving rays, gave to the god of the twelfth month the title of the Doubter. In the Christian calendar this personification is known as Thomas, and a more specific dedication of the shortest day of the year having been made to him, the 21st day of December is called St. Thomas day.

## The seasons

The gods of the seasons were Leo, Taurus, Aquarius and Scorpio. The ancient astrologers substituted Scorpio for the constellation known as Aquila or the Flying Eagle. In the allegorical astronomy of that time these gods of the seasons were designated as animals, and as such we find them referred to in Revelation 4:7, which reads as follows: *"And the first beast was like a lion (Leo), and the second beast like a calf (Taurus, the bull calf), and the third beast had a face as a man, (Aquarius, the waterman) and the fourth beast was like a flying eagle (Aquila)."* In the first chapter of Ezekiel the god of the seasons are referred to in the same manner.

These gods of the seasons, standing, imaginarily, at the four corners of the heavens, were called corner-keepers, and making them witnesses to God Sol in his apparent annual revolution, the founders of the Astral Worship called them Archangels, Evangelists, God-Spellers or Gospel-Bearers, and claiming inspiration from them, composed four different histories of the birth and earth-life of the incarnate savior, to each of which they gave a name, and called these records the gospel story. In its Chaldean version, they were given the names of Gabriel, Michael, Raphael and Uriel; but in the Christian Gospel story they were given the names Matthew, Mark, Luke and John.

## Half year of increasing days

In ancient Astrolatry, the half year of increasing days, extending from the winter to the summer solstice, was personified by the composite figure representing the constellations of Taurus and Aquarius, which was made up of the winged body of a bull and the head and beard of a man, and was called the Cherubim. This personification can be found portrayed on the Assyrian marbles on exhibition in the British Museum.

## Half year of decreasing days

The half year of decreasing days, extending from the summer to the winter solstice, was personified by the figure, which, representing the constellations of Leo and Aquila, and composed of the winged body and limbs of a lion, with the head of an eagle, was called the Seraphim.

These personifications were the Archangels of the ancient astral worship.

## Last quarter of the year

The last quarter of the year was depicted in the ancient allegories as a decrepit old man, who, stung by a scorpion (Scorpio), and fatally wounded by an arrow from the quiver of an archer (Sagittarius) dies at the winter solstice; and, after lying in the grave for three days, is brought to life again. This was the personification referred to in the Christian gospel story as having been raised from the grave by the mandate, "Come forth, Lazarus."

So it becomes obvious that the elders and the saints; the angels, and the archangels; the Cherubim and Seraphim; and also poor old Lazarus, are personifications of the divisions of time.

# Zodiac Symbols of Solar Worship

6

## The Lord of Evil

The founders of ancient astrolatry worshipped the God Sol as Lord of Evil, under the symbol of the serpent, and marked the beginning of his reign by the constellation "Serpens" in conjunction with the autumnal equinox.

## The precession of the equinoxes

After long observation the ancient astrologers discovered that the sun, in making its apparent annual revolution, did not return to the same point in the heavens, but fell behind that of the preceding year, at the, rate of 50 1/4 seconds of a degree annually. At this rate of precession, which modern calculation has confirmed, it requires 71 2-3 years for the cardinal points to pass through one degree on the ecliptic, and 2150 years through thirty degrees, or one sign of the zodiac. With the knowledge of this process providing precise timing, we are able not only to determine the origin of these symbols, but to accurately estimate the dates of their adoption.

## The sphinx

From the teachings of astrology we learn that the summer solstice has passed through three whole periods of 2150 years since it was between the signs of Leo and Virgo. If we multiply 2,150 by 3 we can determine that this took place about 6,450 years ago.

The tourist to the Nile valley can see, near the base of the great Egyptian pyramid Cheops, a colossal head and bust of a woman carved in stone which is attached to a body of a lion in a crouching position. It is 146 feet long, hidden beneath the shifting sands of the desert. When you understand the precession of the equinoxes you can solve the riddle of the sphinx by recognizing in that grotesque monument the mid-summer symbol of solar worship, when the summer solstice was between the signs of Leo and Virgo.

## Dagon

When the summer solstice was between the signs of Leo and Virgo, the winter solstice was between those of Aquarius and Pisces, and the figure composed of the body of a man with the tail of a fish became the mid-winter symbol of solar worship. This was the symbol to which the ancient Phoenicians paid homage to the Lord under the name of Dagon. This mythical creature has since morphed into our notion of a dragon.

## The bull

When the summer solstice entered the sign of Leo, the vernal equinox entered that of Taurus, making the bull the spring symbol of solar worship. The savior was designated in the ancient allegories as the bull of God which takes away the sin of the world; which, in its allegorical sense, signifies the sun in Taurus, or sun of spring, which takes away the evil of winter.

In India this symbol was represented by the figure of a bull with the solar disk between his horns. The Egyptians perpetuated it in their "Apis" or bull deity. The Assyrians represented this symbol by the figure of a winged bull with the face and beard of a man; the Phoenicians, in their "Baal," by the figure of a man with a bull's head and horns. You will also remember it as the golden calf of the ancient Israelites. (Exodus 32)

## The ram

By deducting 2,150 years from 6,450, we can determine

that about 4,300 years ago the vernal equinox entered the sign of Aries, and the spring symbol of solar worship, changing from the bull to the ram, was represented by ram-headed figures, two of which were found in Egypt, and are on exhibition in the British Museum. Then the text which reads the Bull of God was changed to the Ram of God which takes away the sins of the world.

## The lamb

Ultimately attaching a meek and lowly disposition to the imaginary incarnations of the mythical god of the sun, the symbol of the ram was changed to that of the lamb, and the text in the allegories, which read the Ram of God, was changed to read *"The Lamb of God which taketh away the sin of the World,"* John 1:29.

When we understand this it becomes apparent that the originals of the New Testament were composed when the vernal equinox was in the sign of Aries. Having adopted the symbol of the lamb, it was represented by several forms of what is known as Agnus Dei, or Lamb of God, one of which was in the form of a bleeding lamb with a vase attached into which blood is flowing, which originated in reference to the shedding of blood as a symbolic atonement for sin.

But the most comprehensive form of this symbol in its astronomical portrayal was represented by the figure of a lamb in a standing attitude, supporting the circle of the zodiac, divided into quarters to denote the seasons. At each of the cardinal points there was a small cross, and the lamb held in its uplifted fore-foot a larger cross. This symbol is still retained in the Catholic Church.

## The fish

By deducting 2,150 years from 4,300 we determine that about 2,150 years ago the vernal equinox entered the sign of Pisces; and although the original version of the New Testament was founded upon the symbol of the lamb, it is a historical fact that for centuries after the beginning of our era, the Christians paid homage to the Lord under the symbol of the fish; although ultimately going into disuse, the lamb was retained as the distinguishing symbol of the Christian religion until the year 680, when another symbol was substituted, as you will see next.

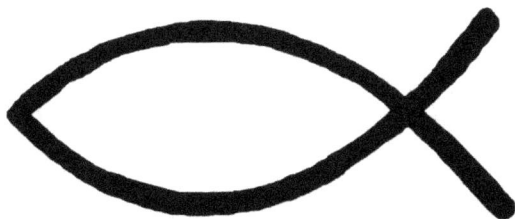

**T Cross - Sign of Taurus**　　　**St. Andrews Cross**

**Ankh**　　　**Nile River Marker**

## Signs of the cross

Among the numerous symbols of solar worship, besides those we have already referred to, there are four which we will examine. Two of these are astronomical symbols: the one adopted when the spring equinox was in the sign of Taurus and shaped like the letter T, was the model after which the ancient temples were built; and the other, shaped like the letter X, in reference to the angle of 23 ½ degrees made by the crossing of the ecliptic and the celestial equator, is known as St. Andrew's Cross.

Two of these are Eqyptian symbols. The similarity between the cross and the Ankh, which is the Egyptian symbol of eternal life, are obvious.

The fourth, and most important of all the symbols of solar worship, in its relation to the Christian religion, which, having no astronomical symbol, originated in Egypt in reference to the annual flooding of the river Nile. To mark the height to which the water should rise to secure an abundant harvest, posts were planted on its banks to which cross beams were attached (forming +). If the water should rise to the designated height, it was called "the waters of life," or "river of life." Ultimately, this form of the cross was adopted as the symbol of the life to come, or eternal life. The ancient astrologers had it engraved on stone, encircled with a hieroglyphic inscription to that effect. One of these engravings was discovered in the ruins of the temple erected at Alexandria, and dedicated to "our Lord and Savior Serapis."

But, if the water failed to rise to the required height starvation became the inevitable result. In this case it was the custom of the people to nail to these crosses symbols of the demon of famine. To indicate the sterility of the domain over which he reigned, he was represented by the figure of a lean and haggard man, with a crown of thorns upon his head. A reed cut from the river's bank was placed in his hands as his scepter. Because of the animosity they felt towards the inhabitants of Judea they put a sign on this figure with the inscription: *This is the King of the Jews.* Thus, to the ancient Egyptians, this sign of the cross was blessed or cursed depending on whether it was represented with or without this figure suspended upon it.

When the Roman, or modern, form of Christianity was instituted, the hieroglyphic inscription signifying the life to come or eternal life was substituted by a sign nailed to the cross with the letters I. N. R. I. inscribed upon it, which are the initials of the Latin words conveying the same meaning. But it was not until the year 680 that the figure of a man suspended upon this form of the cross, came to symbolize Christianity. It was under the Pontificate of Agathon, and during the reign of Constantine Pogonat, at the sixth council of the church, and third at Constantinople, when it was ordered in Canon 82 that *"Instead of a lamb, the figure of a man nailed to a cross should be the distinguishing symbol of the Christian religion."*

As this figure is represented by that of a lean and haggard man, with a crown of thorns upon his head, it becomes obvious that the old Egyptian demon of famine was its model.

# Future Rewards and Punishments

7

In ancient Astrolatry, two different systems of future rewards and punishments were taught. The Oriental or Indian system, which ignored the resurrection of the body, taught that there would be but one judgment immediately after death. The Occidental or Egyptian system taught that there would be an individual judgment immediately after death, the resurrection of the body, and then a general judgment at the end of the world, or conclusion of the 12,000 year cycle.

## The Oriental system

Considering perfect happiness to consist of absolute rest, the Oriental astrologers conceived a state of eternal and unconscious repose, equivalent to soul absorption, to which they gave the name of Nirvana. They taught that, by the awards of the gods, the souls of the righteous, or those who had lived what they called "the contemplative life," would be permitted to enter Nirvana immediately after death. For the souls of sinners, they invented a system of punishments which was known as the Metempsychosis, or transmigration of souls. They taught that souls would be compelled to successively animate the bodies of beasts, birds, fishes, etc.

(reincarnation), for a thousand years before being permitted to enter Nirvana.

## The Occidental system

In coming up with the doctrine of the first judgment the Egyptian astrologers, ignoring the concept of Nirvana, taught that the soul would remain conscious after death. Its rewards and punishments would be enjoyed or suffered in the under or nether world, the existence of which they had developed in constructing their system of nature. This imaginary region, known to the Egyptians as the Amenti, to the Greeks as Hades, and to the Hebrews as Sheol, was divided by an impassable gulf into the two states of happiness and misery which were designated in the Grecian mythology as the Elysium, or Elysian Fields, and the Tartarus. In the lower part of the Tartarus was located the Phlegethon, or lake of fire and brimstone, the smoke from which ascended into an upper chamber.

In this system it was taught that the souls of the two extremes of society (the righteous and the great sinners) would be consigned immediately after the first judgment, the one to the Elysium, and the other to the Phlegethon, where they were to remain until the second or general judgment.

While the souls of less serious sinners, making up the majority of mankind, before being permitted to enter the Elysium would be forced to suffer the punishments of the Metempsychosis, or in the upper region, or "smoky row" of the Tartarus. Such was the Egyptian purgatory, and its occupants were called *"the spirits in prison"* referred to in I Peter 3:19. The priests claimed to have the power to release souls from this prison provided their surviving friends paid liberally for their services. From this concept the clergy of the Catholic church came up with the idea of saying masses for the souls of the dead.

These doctrines were carried by Pythagoras from Egypt to Greece about 550 years before the beginning of our era; and passing from there to Rome, the Greek and Latin poets vied with each other in portraying Hades and the joys and terrors of its two states.

## The second or general judgment

The Egyptian astrologers, recognizing the soul as a material entity, and conceiving the idea that in the future life it would require a physical body for its perfect action, taught that at the general judgment it would be re-united to its resurrected body. In conformity to this belief, Job says in Job 19:25-26, *"I know that my Redeemer liveth, and that he shall stand at the latter day upon the earth; and though worms destroy this body, yet in my flesh shall I see God."*

The higher class Egyptians, however, fearing that their existence would continue to be of the same shadowy and ethereal character after the second judgment, as they believed it would be in the Amenti, if worms were allowed to destroy their bodies, hoped to preserve them until that time by the process of embalming.

The imaginary events to occur in connection with the second judgment, the finale of the plan of redemption, which included what is known as the doctrine of Second Adventism, would begin when an archangel sounding a trumpet summoned the quick and the dead to appear before a panel of the gods to receive their final awards.

At the second judgment, also referred to as "the last day," "day of judgment," "great and terrible day of the Lord," etc., it was taught that the tenth and last savior would come a second time by descending upon the clouds. After the final awards, the chosen ones being caught up *"to meet the Lord in the air"* (1 Thes. 4:17), and the heaven and the earth would be reduced to chaos through fire. That grand catastrophe is recorded in 2 Peter 3:10, that *"the heavens shall pass away with a great noise and the elements shall melt with fervent heat, the earth also and the works that are therein shall be burned up."*

## The millennium

After the organization of a new heaven and a new earth it was taught that there would descend a beautiful city, with pearly gates and golden streets, called the City of God, the Kingdom of God, the Kingdom of Heaven or the New

Jerusalem, in which the redeemed would, with their Lord and savior, enjoy the millennium, or thousand years of happiness without evil. The devotees of astral worship were taught to pray (in what is now known as the Lord's Prayer) for the quick coming of this idyllic kingdom.

According to the teachings of the allegories, there would be no sun, moon or stars during the millennium since the light of those celestial bodies would not be needed. We find recorded in Rev. 21:23, *"The city had no need of the sun, neither of the moon to shine in it; for the glory of God did lighten it,"* and Rev. 22:5, *"there shall be no night there; and they need no candle, neither the light of the sun; for the Lord God giveth them light."*

*"In the early state of society, some wise men insisted on the necessity of darkening truth with falsehood and of persuading men that there is an immortal deity who hears and sees and understands our actions, whatever we may think of that matter ourselves."*

**Euripedes,** a Greek writer
450 BCE.

# 8

# Judeo-Christianity

## The Greeks colonize Alexandria

A system of astral worship, which we now refer to as Judeo-Christianity, was in existence more than two centuries before the churches as we know them began. Historical records tell us that, after the death of Alexander the Great in 332 BCE., the Grecian Empire was divided among his generals. Egypt and its adjacent provinces went to Ptolemy Lagus, or Soter who suppressed a revolt in Judea, and moved a large number of its inhabitants to the new city of Alexandria.

The Greek colonists of Alexandria adopted the Egyptian version of the gospel story as it was more appropriate to the Nile Valley where they currently lived than to Judea where they came from. However they preferred to pay homage to Serapis, the ninth incarnation of God Sol, which they imported from Pontus, a Greek province of Asia Minor. They erected a temple to worship Serapis known as the Grand Serapium.

They introduced the culture and refinement of Greece to the new city. It became, under the Ptolemian dynasty, a great center of learning. The arts and sciences flourished and an immense library was amassed. Various forms of astral worship were represented and schools for the dissemination of the several phases of Grecian philosophy and Oriental Gnosticism were founded.

## The earliest "Christians"

These Jewish residents of Alexandria who adopted the religion of the Greeks, and attached to their incarnate saviors the title signifying "the Christ," or "the anointed one," were known as Christians. Encouraged by the liberal policy of Philadelphus the second Ptolemy, a group of scholars, who had been educated in the Greek schools, founded a college for the education of their own people. This institution became known as the University of Alexandria. The professors of that institution translated their Hebrew sacred records into the Greek language. This translation is known as the Septuagint, or Alexandrian version of the Old Testament.

Having acquired from the Egyptian astrologers the arts of healing, thaumaturgy and necromancy, and teaching these in their school, the professors of the Jewish college of Alexandria assumed the title of Essenes, or Therapeutae, which were the Egyptian and Greek words meaning Doctors, Healers or Wonder Workers. They adopted the "Contemplative Life," or asceticism of the Oriental Gnosticism, from which they derived the name of Ascetics.

Founding a church for the propagation of their beliefs, those who were destined for the ministry assumed the title of Ecclesiastics. Teaching rigid temperance and self-denial among their people, they were known as Enchratites, Nazarites or Abstainers. The more devout among them retired to monasteries, or to the solitude of caves and other secluded places. They were also called Monks, Cenobites, Friars, Eremites, Hermits or Solitaries.

## The 10th incarnation of the God Sol

According to the cyclic teachings of astral worship, the time for the manifestation of the tenth and last incarnation of God Sol had arrived. In other words, it was time to give a new name to the mythical god of the sun. The professors of the Jewish school of Alexandria decided to start their own form of worship. While retaining the same name under which they had worshipped Serapis and had been known as Christians, Essenes or Therapeutae, they substituted for their Christ the name of the Grecian Bacchus, which was composed of the Greek letters IOTA,ETA,SIGMA, signifying Yes, Ies or Jes.

In composing their version of the gospel story, they based it on Serapis and set it in the land of their ancestry. They kept the sign of the cross and the phraseology associated with it although its referral to the Nile River and its annual inundation had no application whatever to the sterile land of Judea. Selecting what they conceived to be the best from other versions of the gospel story, and assuming the title of Eclectics, they designated their system as the Eclectic Philosophy. The asceticism which is derived from the Oriental Gnosticism is perpetuated in the scriptures of modern Christianity.

We also notice that the miracle of converting water into wine, taken from the story of Bacchus, and to the statements that the savior was hung between two thieves was copied from the stories of both Khrishna, the avatar or savior of Indian astrolatry, and the Egyptian god Horus.

Therefore we can see that, although the scene of the gospel story of ancient Christianity was set in the land of Judea, its authors having adopted a Greek version of that story as its basis, given a Greek title and name to their Messiah, perpetuated a Greek name for their sect and quoted exclusively from the Septuagint, or Greek version of the Old Testament, the facts show conclusively that it was not Jews of Judea, but Hellenized Jews of Alexandria, who were the real authors of ancient Christianity.

## The prophecies

The clergy claimed that the prophecies were divine revelations of events yet to occur, and incessantly preached their speedy fulfillment. However, it becomes apparent to anyone looking at how these teachings developed that these scriptures are not the records of future events, divinely revealed, but that they originated with the founders of astral worship, who based them upon predetermined events of their own making.

Regarding the final judgment and the setting up of the kingdom of heaven, which were part of the plan of redemption and from which were derived the doctrines of the second coming, it was decided that these events would occur at the conclusion of the last half of the grand cycle of 12,000 years, which was deemed to be the duration of the human race.

As evidence that the founders of the Jewish or ancient Christianity believed, like the devotees of other forms of astral worship, that the prophecies were soon to be fulfilled, we find that the original version of the New Testament, written by these founders, contains many texts such as:

*"Repent, for the Kingdom of Heaven is at hand."* Matt. 4:17. KJV

*"There be some standing here which shall not taste death till they see the Son of Man coming in His kingdom."* Matt. 16:28. KJV

*"The time is fulfilled, and the Kingdom of God is at hand."* Mark 1:15. KJV

That the original version of the New Testament was composed when the vernal equinox was in the sign of Aries is apparent because it teaches worship of the Lord under the symbol of the lamb. That it was during the last, or 30th degree of that sign, can readily be proven by turning to history which reveals that the Jews were removed from Judea to Alexandria twenty-five years before the accession to the throne of Philadelphus, the Second Ptolemy who, after reigning thirty-nine years, died 246 years before the beginning of the current era.

By turning to the celestial atlas we find that the vernal equinox passed out of the sign of Pisces into that of Aquarius in the year 1900. We have but to deduct that period of time from 2150 (the number of years required for the cardinal points to pass through one whole sign) to determine that the spring equinox passed out of the sign of Aries into that of Pisces 250 years BCE, or about 2,250 years ago. From the projections of astrology we see that the last half of the grand cycle of 12,000 years (which was allotted to man as the duration of his race on earth) would begin at a time corresponding to the autumnal equinox, when that cardinal point was passing out of the sign of Virgo, and that it had to come to an end at a time corresponding to the vernal equinox, when that cardinal point was passing out of the sign of Aries. This explains why, at the last judgment, the office of trumpeter was assigned to the Archangel Gabriel, the genius of spring, and why it was a ram's horn with which he was to blow the ending signal.

## The second coming that didn't come

When the time arrived for the fulfillment of the prophecies we can well imagine that, fearing the wrath of the lamb, there was weeping, wailing and gnashing of teeth among the terror-stricken sinners, while those who believed they had fulfilled their calling were looking with feverish expectancy for the second advent of their Lord and savior. They watched and waited, with ears alert, to hear the sound of Gabriel's trumpet, summoning the quick, and the dead to the general judgment. But not a single blast from the archangel's ram's horn was heard, no Lord appeared descending from Heaven to meet the faithful in the air, and, in the last act of the fearful drama of "judgment day," the curtain refused to be rung down upon a burning world.

With the non-fulfillment of the prophecies, the more enlightened people began to scoff at the priests, who were temporarily demoralized, but soon came up with the explanation that a mistake had been made in the calculations. They came up with an answer for people asking the question *"Where is the promise of his coming? For since the fathers fell asleep, all things continue as they were from the beginning of the creation."* They answered that *"The Lord is not slack concerning His promise,"* but *"as a thief in the night"* he would soon come and all things be fulfilled. See 2 Peter 3.

Further on in history, we find that the founders of modern Christianity, in composing their version of the New Testament from that of the Jewish, or ancient Christians, made no change in its verbiage regarding the prophecies. However, when Constantine I, Emperor of Rome, became the patron of the church, the leaders of the church announced that they had recalculated the time of fulfillment to be the year 1000. History tells us that when the time arrived the whole of Christendom was fearfully agitated about it. Since then every generation has been frustrated with the apparent errors of second Adventism.

By teaching that the prophecies refer to events yet to occur, rather than simply being allegorical stories which explain philosophical concepts, the church perpetuated a massive fraud upon mankind which has flowed through to our present day.

*"Men never do evil so completely and cheerfully as when they do it out of religious conviction."*

**Blaise Pascal,**
French mathematician and philosopher

# 9

# Roman or Modern Christianity

## Religion under Roman rule

In the previous chapter we saw how Judaism, or ancient Christianity, originated at the University of Alexandria, under Greek rule, in this chapter we will see how the modern form of Christianity developed in the same place, but under Roman rule.

In order to understand how Christianity evolved it is important to understand how religion was regarded by Roman society in that era, which was considered the golden age of literature, and produced great thinkers such as Cicero, Tacitus, Pliny, Horace and Virgil. Basically, the Roman leaders considered any form of religion as useful for purposes of control, the people considered every form of religion as equally true, and the philosophers recognized that all religion was essentially just superstition, so religious diversity was not just tolerated, but encouraged.

The Edict of Milan in 313 C.E. reinforced this Roman position regarding religious freedom so that whatever god is entroned in heaven would be well-disposed towards them.

In reference to religion, the English historian Edward Gibbon, in his book *"The Decline and Fall of the Roman Empire"* vol. I., chapter 2, writes:

> *"The policy of the emperors and the senate, as far as it concerned religion, was happily seconded by the reflections of the enlightened, and by the habits of the superstitious, part of their subjects. The various modes of worship, which prevailed in the Roman world, were all considered by the people, as equally true; by the philosopher, as equally false; and by the magistrate, as equally useful. And thus toleration produced not only mutual indulgence, but even religious concord.*
>
> *The superstition of the people was not embittered by any mixture of theological rancor; nor was it confined by the chains of any speculative system. The devout polytheist, though fondly attached to his national rites, admitted with implicit faith the different religions of the earth. Fear, gratitude, and curiosity, a dream or an omen, a singular disorder, or a distant journey, perpetually disposed him to multiply the articles of his belief, and to enlarge the list of his protectors.*
>
> *The thin texture of the Pagan mythology was interwoven with various but not discordant materials. As soon as it was allowed that sages and heroes, who had lived, or who had died for the benefit of their country, were exalted to a state of power and immortality, it was universally confessed that they deserved if not the adoration, at least the reverence of all mankind. The deities of a thousand groves and a thousand streams possessed, in peace, their local and respective influence; nor could the*

Roman who deprecated the wrath of the Tiber, deride the Egyptian who presented his offering to the beneficent genius of the Nile.

The visible powers of Nature, the planets, and the elements, were the same throughout the universe. The invisible governors of the moral world were inevitably cast in a similar mould of fiction and allegory. Every virtue, and even vice, acquired its divine representative; every art and profession its patron, whose attributes, in the most distant ages and countries, were uniformly derived from the character of their peculiar votaries. A republic of gods of such opposite tempers and interest required, in every system, the moderating hand of a supreme magistrate, who, by the progress of knowledge and flattery, was gradually invested with the sublime perfections of an Eternal Parent, and an Omnipotent Monarch.

Such was the mild spirit of antiquity, that the nations were less concerned about the differences than to the similarities of their religious worship. The Greek, the Roman, and the Barbarian, as they met before their respective altars, easily persuaded themselves, that under various names, and with various ceremonies, they adored the same deities. The elegant mythology of Homer gave a beautiful, and almost a regular form, to the polytheism of the ancient world."

At this time the esoteric philosophy, which taught that the gods were mythical and the scriptures allegorical, was widely recognized, so it was understood that it didn't really matter which form of worship you chose as all were equally good.

The University of Alexandria was flourishing at this time. Having ceased to be an exclusively Jewish school, students from all parts of the Roman Empire were attending, and its professors were drawn from the ranks of both Jewish and Gentile scholars.

## Rewriting the scriptures

Realizing the hopelessness of reviving the ancient faith among the upper elements of Roman society who understood the esoteric philosophy, and recognizing that it would be impossible to convert them to a new form of superstition, and understanding the value of religion to mankind (especially to those less educated), these professors chose to institute a system of worship exclusively for the Jews and the lower and neglected classes of Gentiles, which included slaves and criminals. To accomplish this they rewrote the scriptures of the Jewish or ancient Christianity, which had been preserved among the archives of the University.

They made the land of Judea as the location of its version of the gospel story, and added the Latin terminal "us," to the name of its savior, thus making it Iesus or Jesus. Conforming their version of the gospel story to the lowly condition of its expected devotees, they attached to the savior the characteristics of poverty, and taught that he was born in a manger, that his disciples were but humble fishermen and that the poor would be the only elect in the kingdom of heaven.

They incorporated many of the Greek myths, for instance, the Roman letters I. H. S., which is found on crosses in all Catholic churches, is supposed to stand for Jesus Hominum Salvator, or Jesus, Savior of Men, but initially referred to Bacchus the god of wine.

They dropped the names Essene or Therapeutae, and retained the name Christian. They incorporated a thread of real history by arbitrarily making the Christian era begin at the time corresponding to the reign of Augustus. Then they proceeded to destroy the originals from which they compiled their scriptures, and sent out missionaries to all parts of the Empire commissioned to preach salvation only to the lower class Gentiles and to the Jews.

## The Essenes

Much of what is known about the early Christian period comes from the writings of Eusebius of Caesarea, c. 263-339, a church historian of the fourth century. In his book, *"Ecclesiastical History, Book II"* which was originally written in Greek, but has over the centuries been translated into English he explains that the early Christians were Essenes or Therapeutae, and that their writings are our gospels and Epistles. Also, Eusebius refers to the testimony of Philo, and from the writings of Josephus, the Jewish historian, to point out that, at the beginning of the Christian era, the descendants of the ancient Essenes were still observing the practices and customs of monasticism.

It is apparent that the Jews of Judea had no hand in the development of this early Christianity, for, if they had instituted it, they would not have given the Messiah the Greek title signifying the "Christ", but, would have written their version of the Gospel story in their own language, and would have used the Hebrew word signifying the "Shiloh." (See Genesis 49:10)

Furthermore, the Jews were of the belief that the Messiah would manifest himself as a great earthly prince, who would re-establish the throne of David, and deliver them from the oppression of foreign rulers, so they would not have attached to him the humble characteristics of the Christ of the New Testament.

## Roman persecution

So if the Romans were so tolerant of different religions why the famous persecution of Christians that we have all heard about? The Christians brought it on themselves. Believing that their God was the only true God, and that their rituals and beliefs were the only true beliefs they refused to tolerate any other gods to be worshipped and went about attempting to convert other religions and antagonized their leaders.

The Gentile masses, attracted by the promise of enjoying in the world to come the delights denied them in this life, eagerly attached themselves to the new sect, which rapidly increased in numbers. The fanaticism which prevailed among these early Christians was the direct result of their ignorance. Its devotees, seeking the crown of martyrdom, made themselves so obnoxious that they were barely tolerated by the Roman government and suffered death at the hands of the civil authorities.

## Constantine

The Christians were alternately persecuted and tolerated by the Roman Emperors until the first quarter of the fourth century, when the Church of Rome became the recipient of imperial patronage.

Constantine I., also called Constantine the Great (272-337), was the Emperor of Rome from 306 until his death in 337. He had succeeded in making himself sole Emperor by the year 324 by murdering and outmaneuvering all other claimants to the throne.

One version of the events that followed was that Constantine, believing that the lake of fire and brimstone, awaited him in the future life, unless he could obtain absolution for his crimes, became very much distressed. He applied to Sopater, one of the priests of the established religion, for absolution, and was informed that his crimes were so atrocious that there was no absolution for him. One of Constantine's courtiers referred him to the Church of Rome, where he applied to Bishop Silvester for absolution. It was granted and Constantine converted to Christianity. (Note: Constantine didn't seem to have a firm grasp of the concept of Christianity because immediately after his conversion he ordered the death of the priest that had refused to grant him absolution.)

Another version was that since the Christian sect had become a powerful and dangerous faction, Constantine came up with the idea of strengthening his precarious position by professing himself a convert to its tenets. Taking the Church of Rome under his patronage he promoted the bishop to the rank of a prince of the Empire and gave him one of his palaces for a residence.

## The Council of Nicaea

At the time Constantine became the patron of Christianity the bishops and presbyters of the several churches were divided into two factions in discussing the relationship between the Father and the Son. One party, headed by Athanasius, a presbyter of Alexandria, and afterwards bishop, advocated the ancient belief that the three persons in the godhead of Father, Son and Holy Ghost were but one God, that Christ is co-eternal with the Father, and that he became man to perform his mission of redemption. This is what is known as the Athanasian or Trinitarian Creed. The other party, headed, by Arius, another presbyter of Alexandria, advocated the belief in one God alone and that Christ, having no existence until begotten of the Father, is not co-eternal with him. This is what is known as Arianism or Unitarianism.

The faction advocating the Trinitarian creed managed to convert Constantine to their side of the debate, and encouraged him to enforce it as a fundamental doctrine of the Christian theology. So, in 325 Constantine summoned a general council of bishops and priests to meet at Nicaea, in Bithynia, a province of Asia Minor. He presided over their deliberations, clad in gorgeous attire, with a jewel-studded crown, seated upon a gilded chair.

A minority of them, holding to their Arianist beliefs, refused to change their views so he banished them from their positions. The majority adopted the Trinitarian creed, and this majority appealed to Constantine to suppress the writings of Arius. Constantine issued an edict calling for the burning of any book or document espousing this doctrine, and calling for anyone attempting to conceal such a document to be sentenced to death by beheading.

He later readopted the Unitarian faith and restored the banished bishops to their churches. Regardless of his action, the Church of Rome maintained the Trinitarian creed and enforced the dogma of the supreme divinity of Christ.

In spite of his professed conversion to Christianity, Constantine was one of the most brutal tyrants in history. Some of his crimes included scalding his wife to death in a bath of boiling water, and the murdering of six members of his family, one of which was his own son, and yet Constantine was canonized by the Eastern Church.

During the first three centuries, when Christianity was still a weak sect, her bishops begged the tolerance of the Roman Emperors on the ground that their form of worship was virtually the same as the established religion. But after Constantine's conversion its hierarchy began to demand the recognition of Christianity as the state religion. To give their demands more credibility they insisted that their scriptures were really historical, and that there was no resemblance whatever between the two forms of worship; theirs was of Divine authenticity while the pagan religion was purely a human institution.

## Christianity triumphs over the old pagan religion

By the fourth century Christians firmly believed that their scriptures were historical; that Jesus Christ was truly the incarnate savior who had died and rose again for the salvation of mankind, and that it would be just and proper that Christianity be recognized as the state religion.

The conflict raged until the year 381, when, under the reign of the Emperor Theodosius the Great, the Roman Senate, fearing the tumult a refusal would excite, under the pretense of fair dealing ordered the presentation before that Senate, of the respective merits of the two forms of worship. In that presentation, which lasted a whole week, Symmachus, a Senator, advocated for the old system, and Ambrose, the Bishop of Milan, advocated for Christianity. The result was a foregone conclusion, Christianity was decreed the official state religion.

## The split between Trinitarianism and Unitarianism

For centuries after the Council of Nicaea the peace and harmony of the church continued to be disturbed by the same old debate between Trintarianism and Unitarianism. The Western church adhering to Trinitarianism, while the majority of the Eastern congregations maintained their faith in Unitarianism.

Ultimately the Trinitarian believers grew stronger and began persecuting the followers of the Unitarian faith, and by the sixth century many of whom moved into northern Arabia where they founded numerous monasteries and impressed their Unitarian faith upon the Arab people. Unitarianism was ultimately incorporated into the Koran, the sacred book of Islam; and followers of that form of worship retained the belief that Christ was but one of the prophets.

## Discovering the lost tomb of the savior

Knowing that it would be great for validating the gospel story as a literal history if they could have a tomb of the savior to which pilgrimages could be made; the church hierarchy asked Constantine if he could provide one. So he sent his mother, Helena, to Judea to find the place and not surprisingly she found it. Constantine then erected, over the designated spot, the church of the Holy Sepulcher which remains to this day.

Helena, apparently good at finding lost things, also claimed to have discovered the actual cross upon which the Savior had been crucified, and the robes he was wearing.

## Conquering under the sign of the cross

According to Eusebius, upon learning that his mother Helena had found the cross upon which Jesus had been crucified, Constantine claimed that he had seen with his own eyes a cross of light in the heavens, above the sun, bearing the inscription: "In Hoc Signo Vinces," signifying "Under this sign, conquer."

With the new religion firmly established the vengeful bishops ruthlessly murdered the priests of the old religion, and seized its temples, demolishing some and converting others into churches. They destroyed some of the statues representing the ancient divinities, or, after mutilation, exposed others in public places to the derision of the people. They designated the followers of the older form of worship infidels and exposed them to persecution. They destroyed their works of art, burned their libraries, suppressed their schools of learning, either killed or exiled their professors, and decreed the destruction of all books antagonistic to Christianity.

Among the murders perpetrated in Alexandria in the name of Christianity was that of Hypatia, the beautiful and accomplished daughter of Theon, who had succeeded her father as professor of mathematics and philosophy in the Alexandrian University. In the year 415, while on her way to deliver a lecture she was dragged from her chariot and murdered by order of Bishop Cyril.

# The Dark Ages

The onslaught of Christian savagery obliterated the civilizations of Greece and Rome, and began the long reign of intellectual night known as the Dark Ages.

The justification for destroying the art, temples and documents of the old religion was that by doing so they were preventing the infidels from persevering in their errors.

Little emphasis was placed on the value of education even among the clergy. Johann Lorenz von Mosheim, (1693-1755) wrote in his book *"Ecclesiastical History; Vol. 4"* part 2, chap. 1, says: *"It is certain that the greatest part both of the bishops and presbyters were men entirely destitute of learning and education."*

In the ninth century, Alfred the Great of England lamented that there was, at that time, not a priest in his dominions who understood Latin; and for many centuries afterward the bishops and priests of the whole Christian community were unable to even write their own names and instead they signed documents by the sign of the cross.

## The sabbath

In ancient astral worship it was taught that God Sol was engaged in the reorganization of chaos during the first six periods of the twelve thousand year cycle, corresponding to the months of spring and summer. They also taught that he rested from his labors on the seventh period, corresponding to the first of the autumn months. Observing the apparent period of winter rest in nature, they taught that God ordained the seventh day of the week as the sabbath or rest day for man.

The founders of ancient Judaism enforced the observance of the seventh day sabbath in the fourth commandment of the Decalogue, which, found in Exodus 20:8-11 reads:

> *"Remember the sabbath day, to keep it holy. Six days shalt thou labour, and do all thy work: But the seventh day is the sabbath of the LORD thy God: in it thou shalt not do any work, thou, nor thy son, nor thy daughter, thy manservant, nor thy maidservant, nor thy cattle, nor thy stranger that is within thy gates: For in six days the LORD made heaven and earth, the sea, and all that in them is, and rested the seventh day: wherefore the LORD blessed the sabbath day, and hallowed it."*

Thus the seventh day of the week was made the sabbath of the Old Testament; but it is apparent that the authors of the New Testament, ignored its observance, as may be seen by reference to Mark 2:23: *"And it came to pass, that he went through the corn fields on the sabbath day; and his disciples began, as they went, to pluck the ears of corn."*

Mark 2:27 *"And he said unto them, the sabbath was made for man, and not man for the sabbath."*

John 5:2-18 describes how Jesus healed a man on the sabbath.

Romans 14:5 states it very clearly: *"One man esteemeth one day above another: another esteemeth every day alike. Let every man be fully persuaded in his own mind."*

Col. 2:16; *"Let no man therefore judge you in meat, or in drink, or in respect of a holyday, or of the new moon, or of the sabbath days."*

After Constantine's conversion to Christianity the hierarchy of the church appealed to the Emperor to give them a sabbath, and although they knew that the seventh day of the week was the sabbath of the Old Testament, and that Sunday was the first of the six working days, according to the fourth commandment, their hatred to the Jews for refusing to accept their Christ as the Savior induced them to have it placed on the first day of the week. So, in the year 321, Constantine declared that all townspeople and tradesmen should rest on the venerable day of the Sun. However, those who live in the country were free to go about the tending of their fields and livestock.

Thus we see that the primary movement towards enforcing the observance of the sabbath did not originate in a Divine command, but in the edict of an earthly Emperor. This edict was ratified at the Third Council of Orleans, in the year 538. The Church of Rome began to enforce the observance of the day. It was not until the 12th century that its observance had become so universal as to receive the designation of "The Christian Sabbath."

Once you are aware of how Sunday became the sabbath it is obvious that it is entirely a human institution.

## The Council of Constantinople

During the 6th century of the Christian era the bishops came up with the previously unheard of doctrine of preexistence of spirit. God was declared to be purely a spiritual deity, who existed before matter and created the universe from nothing. Being the sole custodians of the scriptures they changed the six periods of a thousand years each to the six days of creation. They altered Genesis 1:1, to read, *"In the beginning God created the heaven and the earth,"* which in the original read: *"In the beginning, when the Gods (Elohim or Alehim) had made (shaped or formed) this heaven and this earth."*

Making these changes required other changes to be made. They made two distinct and independent beings of the principles of good and evil personified in the God Sol; the former they embodied in Jesus the Christ and the latter in the Christian Devil, thus replacing old Pluto, the presiding god of the underworld.

Rejecting the ancient doctrines regarding the soul, and teaching that, having come from a purely spiritual deity, it would exist eternally as an independent spiritual entity, they substituted the ancient system of limited rewards and punishments for one teaching their endless duration.

These changes in the creed, which were confirmed at the general council of Constantinople, in the year 553, required further changes in the scriptures. The righteous were promised "eternal life" in the Paradise of God beyond the stars; while condemning great sinners to "everlasting punishment" in the Tartarian fires of the underworld, the less serious sinners were to do penance in the same old Purgatory.

Thus, having invented an endless heaven and an endless hell for purely spiritual souls, and neglecting to remove the doctrines of the resurrection of the body, the setting up of the kingdom of heaven on a reorganized earth and other materialistic teachings of the ancient religion, they made the scriptures a combination of things old and new.

## Martin Luther and the Protestant Reformation

The idea that sinners could be sprung from purgatory through donations to the church proved to be a big money maker for the church. People could prepay for their lesser sins during this life, or their loved ones could pay for them afterward, known as paying for indulgences. There is an old saying that is attributed to the German fundraising priest and indulgence salesman Johann Tetzel (1465-1519) that goes "As soon as the coin in the coffer rings, the soul from purgatory springs."

Initially objecting to the selling of indulgences a German priest named Martin Luther wrote *"The Ninety-Five Theses"* in 1517. He believed that forgiveness of sin was not a result of good works (of which paying money to the church was one method), but that it was a gift from God through his son Jesus. This was pretty much the beginning of the concept of vicarious atonement through the blood of Jesus Christ which most Evangelical churches teach today. He refused to recant his position which ultimately resulted in his being excommunicated by Pope Leo X in 1520.

Martin Luther translated the Bible from the Latin into German making it available to the common people. Of course, by this time the scriptures had been modified so much, and their true origins clouded, that it was difficult to know what had originally been written.

While the idea of questioning the doctrines of the Roman Catholic Church would seem to be a good thing, the Reformation ushered in one of the darkest periods in religious history, as we will see later on in this book.

*"Obviously, you have to regard with deep suspician any group or movement, however noble its declarations, that proceeds to win its case by silencing, excommunicating, or murdering its assumed opponents."*

**Tom Harpur,**
retired Anglican priest
professor of New Testament studies
and author of *"The Pagan Christ"*

# 10

## Druidism and Freemasonry

### Druidism

Druidism was a form of astral worship observed by ancient people worldwide. Its ceremonies took place outdoors in consecrated groves and emphasized a reverence for the natural world.

Later, as other forms of astral worship evolved, Druidism existed primarily in northern Europe, particularly among the Scandinavian and Germanic races, and by the inhabitants of Gaul and the British Isles.

The term Druid did not mean only priest, but encompassed all members of the learned class. It was an oral tradition passed on through stories, so no written records remain to confirm exactly what was taught, but the principal point of their doctrine was a belief in reincarnation, the belief that the soul does not die and that after death it passes from one body into another.

Druidism was outlawed by the Roman government from the 3rd century on but pockets of believers existed in hiding in Britain. In the year 596 Pope Gregory I sent Augustin, and forty other monks of the order of St. Andrew, from Rome to Britain, to convert the natives to Christianity. As Christianity moved across Europe when one of the reigning kings became a "convert" to Christianity the whole of his subjects were baptized into the Church of Rome by Imperial decree. The Anglo-Saxons (the Germanic tribes in the south and east of Britain) embraced the new faith, but the Britons (the Celtic peoples in the north and west of Britain) rejected it, and, being persecuted by the Christians, fled primarily to the area now known as Wales, where they observed Druidism in secret for centuries.

**Freemasonry**

While the Northern European Druids still observed their religious ceremonies outdoors, the Egyptians, Assyrians, Indians, Greeks, and Romans began observing their religious services in temples.

After the fifth century Roman edict decreeing the death penalty against all persons discovered practicing any of the rites and ceremonies of the ancient religion, a group of its adherents, banded together to observe the old religion in secrecy.

In an attempt to mask their real object, they took advantage of the fact that while the square and compass, the plumb line, etc., were symbols of speculative masonry in the temple form of astral worship, they publicly claimed to be only a trades-union for the promotion of the arts of architecture and masonry. Among themselves they were known as Free and Accepted Masons or Freemasons. In accordance with the ancient mysteries they instituted lower and higher degrees; in the former they taught the Exoteric creed, and in the latter the Esoteric philosophy. The candidates for initiation were subjected to ceremonies representing the figurative death and resurrection of the Sun god, and were required to take oaths not to reveal the secrets of the order. To enable them to recognize each other, and to render aid to a brother in emergencies, they adopted a system of grips, signs and calls.

To guard against the intrusion of their Christian enemies they stationed watchmen outside of their lodges to warn of their approach. Recognizing the true object of Freemasonry, the hierarchy of the Church of Rome resolved to suppress them, and they were forced to go into hiding until the conclusion of the Dark Ages, when the Reformation made it possible for a form of the order to be revived among the Protestants.

It is apparent that while Freemasonry was a perpetuation of the temple form of astral worship, and while some of its symbols are as old as the ancient Egyptian religion, it did not form as a secret order until Christian persecution in the 5th century made it necessary.

## Masonic symbolism

Looking at the Masonic symbolism it is obvious that Freemasonry is based on the temple worship of ancient Egypt.

THE MASONIC ARMS

From previous chapters we recognize the significance of the sun and moon, and the seven stars. We see the constellation Sirius (or Dog-star, worshipped by the Egyptians under the name of Anubis), whose rising warned the Egyptian people of the rising of the Nile River.

We see the seven signs of the zodiac from Aries to Libra, through which the sun was supposed to pass in making its annual revolution, and which constitutes the Royal Arch from which was derived the name of one of Freemasonry's higher degrees.

The pictures of the Lion, the Bull, the Waterman, and the Flying Eagle, which represent the zodiac signs at the cardinal points, signified the gods of the seasons.

The checkered flooring or mosaic work on the floors of Masonic temples, which was introduced when temple worship replaced the earlier grove form of worship, represents the earth and its variegated face.

The two columns represent the imaginary pillars of heaven resting upon the earth supporting the Royal Arch.

The letter "G" stands for Geometry, the knowledge of which was of great importance to the natives of Egypt in establishing the boundaries of their lands which fluctuated according to the force of the Nile floodwaters.

The square and compass, being the instruments through which the old landmarks were restored, and which ultimately became symbols of justice.

The cornucopia, or horn of plenty, denoted the sun in the sign of Capricorn, and indicated the season when the harvest was gathered and provisions laid up for winter use.

The cenotaph or mock coffin with the sign of the cross upon its lid referred to the sun's crossing of the celestial equator at the autumnal equinox, and to the figurative death of the sun god in the lower hemisphere whose resurrection at the vernal equinox is symbolized by the sprig of acacia sprouting near the head of the coffin.

The serpent, poking out from the small container to the left, represented the symbol of the Lord of Evil under whose control was placed the seasons of autumn and winter.

The figure of a box at the right hand represented the sacred ark in which the symbols of solar worship were deposited.

# Creation Myths

11

## How did the world begin?

How the world began is one of the universal questions of mankind. The Bible does not contain the only creation story, and certainly not the oldest one. Almost every society has a creation story that describes their earliest beginnings, how the world began, and how mankind first came into it. These stories express what the society considers to be profound truths through metaphor and imagery.

Certain features are found in all creation myths. They usually describe how the world developed from a state of chaos or formlessness by a human-like deity or an animal with human characteristics.

Christian believers who insist that the Bible is the divinely inspired word of God usually do not realize (or manage to ignore) that it contains two very different creation stories.

# First version Genesis 1:1-2:3 KJV

In this account, God creates the world over a series of six days by divine command.

## Day 1 - God says "Let there be light!" and light is created.

*Genesis 1*

*1 In the beginning God created the heaven and the earth.*

*2 And the earth was without form, and void; and darkness was upon the face of the deep. And the Spirit of God moved upon the face of the waters.*

*3 And God said, Let there be light: and there was light.*

*4 And God saw the light, that it was good: and God divided the light from the darkness.*

*5 And God called the light Day, and the darkness he called Night. And the evening and the morning were the irst day.*

## Day 2 - God separates the waters, and creates heaven and earth.

*6 And God said, Let there be a firmament in the midst of the waters, and let it divide the waters from the waters.*

*7 And God made the firmament, and divided the waters which were under the firmament from the waters which were above the firmament: and it was so.*

*8 And God called the firmament Heaven. And the evening and the morning were the second day.*

## Day 3 - God creates the seas and the dry land and fills the earth with vegetation.

*9 And God said, Let the waters under the heaven be gathered together unto one place, and let the dry land appear: and it was so.*

*10 And God called the dry land Earth; and the gathering together of the waters called he Seas: and God saw that it was good.*

*11 And God said, Let the earth bring forth grass, the herb yielding seed, and the fruit tree yielding fruit after his kind, whose seed is in itself, upon the earth: and it was so.*

*12 And the earth brought forth grass, and herb yielding seed after his kind, and the tree yielding fruit, whose seed was in itself, after his kind: and God saw that it was good.*

*13 And the evening and the morning were the third day.*

## Day 4 - God puts lights in the sky to separate day from night and creates the seasons.

*14 And God said, Let there be lights in the firmament of the heaven to divide the day from the night; and let them be for signs, and for seasons, and for days, and years:*

*15 And let them be for lights in the firmament of the heaven to give light upon the earth: and it was so.*

*16 And God made two great lights; the greater light to rule the day, and the lesser light to rule the night: he made the stars also.*

*17 And God set them in the firmament of the heaven to give light upon the earth,*

*18 And to rule over the day and over the night, and to divide the light from the darkness: and God saw that it was good.*

*19 And the evening and the morning were the fourth day.*

## Day 5 - God creates sea creatures and birds and commands them to multiply.

*20 And God said, Let the waters bring forth abundantly the moving creature that hath life, and fowl that may fly above the earth in the open firmament of heaven.*

*21 And God created great whales, and every living creature that moveth, which the waters brought forth abundantly, after their kind, and every winged fowl after his kind: and God saw that it was good.*

*22 And God blessed them, saying, Be fruitful, and multiply, and fill the waters in the seas, and let fowl multiply in the earth.*

*23 And the evening and the morning were the fifth day.*

**Day 6 - God creates land creatures. Man and woman are created last, after the entire world is prepared for them; both of them are created in the "image" of God, and given dominion and care over all other created things.**

*24 And God said, Let the earth bring forth the living creature after his kind, cattle, and creeping thing, and beast of the earth after his kind: and it was so.*

*25 And God made the beast of the earth after his kind, and cattle after their kind, and every thing that creepeth upon the earth after his kind: and God saw that it was good.*

*26 And God said, Let **us** make man in **our** image, after **our** likeness: and let them have dominion over the fish of the sea, and over the fowl of the air, and over the cattle, and over all the earth, and over every creeping thing that creepeth upon the earth.* (note the use of the words "us" and "our" indicating more than one god)

*27 So God created man in his own image, in the image of God created he him; male and female created he them.*

*28 And God blessed them, and God said unto them, Be fruitful, and multiply, and replenish the earth, and subdue it: and have dominion over the fish of the sea, and over the fowl of the air, and over every living thing that moveth upon the earth.*

*29 And God said, Behold, I have given you every herb bearing seed, which is upon the face of all the earth, and every tree, in the which is the fruit of a tree yielding seed; to you it shall be for meat.*

*30 And to every beast of the earth, and to every fowl of the air, and to every thing that creepeth upon the earth, wherein there is life, I have given every green herb for meat: and it was so.*

*31 And God saw every thing that he had made, and, behold, it was very good. And the evening and the morning were the sixth day.*

## Day 7 - God rested on the seventh and final day of creation

*Genesis 2*

*1 Thus the heavens and the earth were finished, and all the host of them.*

*2 And on the seventh day God ended his work which he had made; and he rested on the seventh day from all his work which he had made.*

*3 And God blessed the seventh day, and sanctified it: because that in it he had rested from all his work which God created and made.*

Notice that in this version man and woman are created last, after the entire world is prepared for them. Both man and woman are created in the "image" of God, and given dominion over all other created things.

They are told that they can eat every fruit or seed in the world. Does this mean that God is telling them to be vegetarians?

# The second version Genesis 2:4 - 2:25

In the second story it does not say how long creation took. This version does not specify a period of seven days, and it has a very different description of how woman was created.

Where it says, *"In the day that the LORD God made the earth and the heavens,"* the author is using an expression like "during the time" or as we might say "back in my day." It seems obvious that it does not mean an actual literal 24 hour period because it does not mention any reference toward time for the remaining activities.

> *4 These are the generations of the heavens and of the earth when they were created, in the day that the LORD God made the earth and the heavens,*

> *5 And every plant of the field before it was in the earth, and every herb of the field before it grew: for the LORD God had not caused it to rain upon the earth, and there was not a man to till the ground.*

> *6 But there went up a mist from the earth, and watered the whole face of the ground.*

## God creates man

In this version, the creation of man comes after the creation of the heavens and earth, but before the creation of other plants and animals. Man is formed from the dust of the ground, and God breathes life into him.

> *7 And the LORD God formed man of the dust of the*

*ground, and breathed into his nostrils the breath of life;*
*and man became a living soul.*

## God creates the Garden of Eden

God creates the Garden of Eden for man and fills it
with plants and trees bearing fruit for him to eat.

*8 And the LORD God planted a garden eastward in*
*Eden; and there he put the man whom he had formed.*

*9 And out of the ground made the LORD God to grow*
*every tree that is pleasant to the sight, and good for food;*
*the tree of life also in the midst of the garden, and the tree*
*of knowledge of good and evil.*

*10 And a river went out of Eden to water the garden; and*
*from thence it was parted, and became into four heads.*

*11 The name of the first is Pison: that is it which*
*compasseth the whole land of Havilah, where there is gold;*

*12 And the gold of that land is good: there is bdellium*
*and the onyx stone.*

*13 And the name of the second river is Gihon: the same is*
*it that compasseth the whole land of Ethiopia.*

*14 And the name of the third river is Hiddekel: that is*
*it which goeth toward the east of Assyria. And the fourth*
*river is Euphrates.*

*15 And the LORD God took the man, and put him into*

*the garden of Eden to dress it and to keep it.*

## The man is told that he can eat the fruit of any tree but one

*16 And the LORD God commanded the man, saying, Of every tree of the garden thou mayest freely eat:*

*17 But of the tree of the knowledge of good and evil, thou shalt not eat of it: for in the day that thou eatest thereof thou shalt surely die.*

## God makes companions for man

Birds and animals are created as man's companions and helpers. Man gives names to each one, but decides that none are suitable to be his helper.

*18 And the LORD God said, It is not good that the man should be alone; I will make him an help meet for him.*

*19 And out of the ground the LORD God formed every beast of the field, and every fowl of the air; and brought them unto Adam to see what he would call them: and whatsoever Adam called every living creature, that was the name thereof.*

*20 And Adam gave names to all cattle, and to the fowl of the air, and to every beast of the field; but for Adam there was not found an help meet for him.*

## God creates woman

God puts Adam to sleep and removes one of his ribs, which he uses to make the first woman.

*21 And the LORD God caused a deep sleep to fall upon Adam, and he slept: and he took one of his ribs, and closed up the flesh instead thereof;*

*22 And the rib, which the LORD God had taken from man, made he a woman, and brought her unto the man.*

*23 And Adam said, This is now bone of my bones, and flesh of my flesh: she shall be called Woman, because she was taken out of Man.*

*24 Therefore shall a man leave his father and his mother, and shall cleave unto his wife: and they shall be one flesh.*

*25 And they were both naked, the man and his wife, and were not ashamed.*

As we will see later in this book, this version of the creation story has been used as the justification for the denigration of women since the beginning of the Christian era.

## Creation myths that predate the Bible

Almost every civilization had some form of creation myth, many of which predate the Judeo-Christian version. Unlike the Bible version, most recognize the importance or the equality of both male and female, the gods are married, and they procreate. There is also usually a sense of partnership between man, animals, and the earth, rather than a sense that man is the boss and everything else is under his control.

## Babylonian creation myth

The Babylonian creation myth, the **Enûma Elish**, dates to the late second millennium BCE (somewhere between 1700-1900 BCE) or earlier.

This creation myth explains how the world was created, how the god Marduk became the primary god, and why mankind was created. It is a very long soap opera like family feud story, but the short version goes something like this, initially the world was a watery abyss and there were two primeval gods, a saltwater ocean goddess named Tiamat, and her husband, a freshwater god named Apsû. They create other gods (children gods who live in Tiamat's body). These gods create so much noise and havoc that they really annoy the parents and disrupt their sleep to the point that the father god Apsû wants to kill them. (What parent can't relate to this story!)

The most powerful of the children gods kills Apsû and this turns the ocean goddess against them. Now all of the children gods are under the threat of attack from the mother/ocean goddess Tiamat, so they turn to a grandson god Marduk for help. He agrees to fight Tiamat as long as the other gods agree to appoint him as their leader. The other gods agree to Marduk's conditions, and Marduk fights his grandmother Tiamat and kills her. He rips her corpse in two and with the two pieces he makes the earth and the skies. Next he organizes the planets, stars, the moon, sun, and controls the weather. He then creates Babylon as the earthly counterpart to the realm of the gods and kills Tiamat's new husband to prevent his taking revenge, and uses the blood to create humankind so that they may become the servants of the gods.

## Ancient Egyptian creation myths

There were at least three separate creation myths in Egyptian mythology.

Egyptian mythology is an enormous field of study, so obviously this is not intended to cover the entire field, but I want to present a few examples that show how, unlike Christianity, these ancient Egyptian myths emphasize the importance of both male and female, the complementary nature of opposites.

## The Ennead

The Ennead was the story of a family grouping of nine deities consisting of the sun god Atum, his children Shu and Tefnut, the grandchildren Geb and Nut and the great grandchildren Osiris, Set, Isis, and Nephthys.

In this story the first god Atum arose from the primordial waters and masturbated because he was alone and did not have a partner. His semen produced Tefnut, representing moisture, and Shu representing dryness. This ancient Egyptian concept of something good coming from masturbation is in stark contrast with the emphasis on the evil nature of the body and sexuality in the Judeo-Christian tradition.

Shu and Tefnut mated and created Geb (the earth), and Nut (the sky). Then Geb and Nut mated and created Osiris (death), Set (desert), Isis (life), and Nephthys (fertile land).

## The Ogdoad

In this myth eight deities, in four female-male pairs create the world and everything in it. Each pair represents one of the four original states, water, air, darkness, and eternity. Their interactions are initially harmonious, but they become unbalanced, throwing the world into turmoil resulting in the arising of a new entity, death.

It all began when an egg was laid by a celestial bird, an ibis. The sun god Ra developed from this egg. Then Ra created Hathor, his wife, and they had a son Horus who was married to Isis.

## Ptah, speaking the world into existence

This third myth was closer to the Bible version of creation in that the god Ptah was thought to be eternal and everlasting, and his spoken word was what created the world and all the gods into existence.

## Classical Greek creation myths

The classical Greek creation story contains many of the elements of the ancient Babylonian creation myth. In the beginning there was only chaos or nothingness. This chaos gave birth to the goddess Gaea (the earth), and a number of other gods.

On her own Gaea created the god Oranos (the starry sky), and the god Pontus (the sea). Then she had sex with Oranos and gave birth to six male gods and six female gods.

At her urging, Gaea's son Cronos castrated his father and married his sister Rhea and became the ruler of the gods. They had a number of children including Zeus, Poseidon, and Hades, who then overthrew their father as ruler. The three drew lots to determine what portion of the world each of them would rule. Zeus drew the sky, Poseidon the sea and Hades the underworld.

It seems that ever since the earliest times people have been fascinated by tales of intrigue, betrayal, and incest.

## Eridu Genesis - the oldest documented creation myth

One of the oldest known creation myths, the Sumerian creation myth, was found on a fragmentary clay tablet which was discovered in Nippur which is located in the modern day city of Nuffar in Iraq. This tablet was written in the Summarian language and is referred to as the "Eridu Genesis." Eridu was one of the first Sumerian cities believed to be founded by the gods.

Sumerian civilization was one of the earliest known civilizations in the world spanning close to 4000 years, from approximately 6000 to 2000 BCE, and as the birthplace of writing, the wheel, the arch, year round cultivation of land, and irrigation systems, it is considered the *"Cradle of Civilization."*

There are pieces missing from this tablet, but basically, in this myth four gods, Anu the sky god, Enlil the god of wind, Enki the god of water, and Ninhursanga the earth or mother goddess, create the world and everything in it.

Like the Christian Bible it also includes a flood myth.

Basically, the story is that the gods are disappointed with their creation and decide to send a great flood to destroy all of mankind. However, the god of the waters warns the hero, a man known for his humility and obedience, and gives him instructions for building a boat so that he and his family can survive the flood and save all the animals from extinction.

Once the boat is completed and all the animals are on board, a terrible storm ensues and the boat rides out the storm for seven days and seven nights, before Utu the sun god appears and ends the storm.

The Sumerian flood legend was written on this tablet somewhere around 1800 BCE but the story itself would have been composed several thousand years earlier, while the flood story in the Bible was written somewhere between 1450 and 450 BCE. Flood myths with many similarities to the Sumerian story appear in many other cultures long before the Bible was written.

## Norse & Germanic

In the ancient Norse creation story, in the beginning there was nothing but ice in the north, and fire in the south. In between was a void where a few sparks of fire melted a few pieces of ice and created moisture. The evil frost giant Ymir grew out of this moisture. He was alone at first, but then as he slept the sweat from under his arms created two more giants, one male and one female. Then one of his legs mated with the other to create a third giant.

These frost giants were nursed by a giant cow that was created from the melting ice. As this giant cow licked a block of salty ice her licking sculpted the block of ice into the shape of a man which became the frost giant Buri.

## The Norse flood story

The giant Buri fathered a son Borr, who fathered three sons, the gods Vili, Ve, and Odin. The three brothers killed the evil giant Ymir, whose blood resulted in a vast flood which killed all the frost giants except those who floated safely in a hollow tree.

Odin and his two brothers used the evil frost giant's body to create the universe. They ground his flesh into dirt. His bones became the mountains, his teeth rocks and pebbles, then they threw his brains into the sky to create the clouds, and took sparks and embers from the southern fire for the sun, moon and stars.

Then the three gods created the first human beings from fallen trees.

# Creation myths in the new world

The inhabitants of the new world had their own creation myths, oral traditions passed down since the beginning of time. Many of these stories emphasized teamwork and the interdependence of humans and animals.

## Cherokee

According to the Cherokee creation story, in the beginning, there was just water. All the animals lived above it in the sky which was becoming seriously overcrowded. One day a water beetle, volunteered to explore the expanse of water to see if he could find a place for them to live. He explored beneath the surface and brought back mud from the bottom which began to grow and spread outward until it formed land.

Then the other animals attached this new land to the sky with four strings, creating a large expanse of land making space for all of them.

## Lakota

In the Lakota creation story the gods lived in the underworld and humans were their servants. Spider, the trickster, caused a falling-out in the heavens between the sun god and his wife the moon. Their estrangement resulted in the creation of day and night.

Spider then sent a wolf into the underworld to convince people to travel to the surface for a visit, telling them about the beautiful world aboveground. When they emerged through a cave (Wind Cave in the Black Hills), they found the world to be strikingly beautiful, but they soon discovered that they had been tricked, and that life on the Earth was full of hardship, but by then they were unable to return below ground.

## Incan

Unlike many of the creation stories in the new world which were strictly oral traditions, the Incan creation story was recorded by priests, and illustrated on art and pottery.

According to these accounts, in ancient times the earth was covered in darkness. The god Con Tiqui Viracocha emerged out of Lake Titicaca and brought some human beings with him. He created the sun, the moon, and the stars to light the world. Con Tiqui created more human beings from rocks and sent these people off to populate the world.

As in the story of the Garden of Eden, the creator filled the earth with good things to supply all the needs of the first people, but the people rebelled so the creator punished them by stopping the rainfall. The people were then forced to work hard. Then in a twist suggestive of evolution, a new god, Pachacamac, came and drove the first creator out and changed the first people into monkeys. Pachacamac then took over the earth and created the ancestors of modern human beings. But the story doesn't end there, it goes on to tell a story of jealousy, greed, betrayal, sibling rivalry, and murder.

## Are creation myths really necessary?

So it would seem that most cultures and religions have developed some form of creation myth. But are they really necessary, and are we really expected to believe that they are depictions of actual events?

Buddhism is the one religion that generally ignores questions regarding the origin of life because it recognizes that it is pointless to speculate about something that is unknowable. To speculate about the origin of life does not lead to the goal of attaining Nirvana or enlightenment.

The Buddha compared such speculation to the parable of the poison arrow: if a man is shot with a poison arrow, but before he allows the doctor to pull it out he insists on knowing who shot it (arguing the existence of God), where the arrow came from (where the universe came from) and why the person shot it (why God created the universe), then the man will die before the arrow is pulled out.

Since in Buddhism there is no creation myth, there has never been a conflict between Buddhism and science since science is considered to be a complementary means of understanding the world around us.

*"We must remember that the main purpose of the trial and execution is not to save the soul of the accused but to achieve the public good and put fear into others."*

**Francisco Pena**
Inquisitor 1578

# The Dark Side of Religion

# 12

For a religion claiming to bring peace and love to all it touches, Christianity certainly has fallen short of its professed goals throughout its history.

## Dissention made illegal

Once Christianity became the official religion of the Roman Empire it became illegal to question or disagree with the Church. In 388 a law was passed making public discussion of religious topics illegal, and any form of pagan worship was considered a criminal activity. Pagan temples were looted and destroyed. If Christians wanted to seize any assets they simply had to claim that pagan ceremonies were being performed there and they had the right to go in and loot and destroy. The great library of Alexandria was destroyed in 391 and an estimated 700,000 documents were destroyed.

## The Dark Ages

When the Christian church assumed leadership all study in the fields of medicine, science, history, and art was seen as heresy. Ignorance became a virtue. The Christian church's burning of books and repression of intellectual pursuit sent civilization into decline that lasted for the next 1000 years. All of the technological advancements of the previous two thousand years were gradually lost. What little education was available was controlled by the church and limited to the clergy.

## Re-writing history

It wasn't enough that they destroyed all ancient literature and historical documents, and put an end to all actual historical research, the church began re-writing history to suit its purposes. History was rewritten to make the Bible appear to be an accurate historical record rather than just a series of allegorical stories.

Scientific evidence over the past 200 years has shown that the earth is far older than the 6000 or so years that the Christian church wants us to believe. Radiometric age dating indicates that the earth is at least 4 billion years old.

## The church's effect on the world of art

Art was to enhance and promote Christian values. Anything thought to oppose these Christian values was to be desecrated or destroyed. From the 5th century until approximately the 15th century the only acceptable art consisted of depictions of Bible stories or the lives of the saints. Art became teaching aids for the illiterate rather than a thing of beauty or a form of personal expression.

## The church's devastating effect on the economy

Using the story of Jesus overturning the money changers' tables in the temple as justification, the church frowned upon the charging of interest. This made it very difficult to fund business ventures. They discouraged any kind of trade in which they were not profiting. If it was to the church's benefit they would intervene in contractual agreements between outside parties and cancel contracts. In effect, the church was the only organization allowed to make a profit, and as a result it amassed incredible wealth.

Individuals striving for money and power found the church to be the most potentially lucrative career available during the Dark Ages and, in a church that claimed to extol virtues of poverty, many clergymen became extremely wealthy.

Since the story of Adam and Eve put the blame for mankind's downfall on Eve, women had always been looked down on by the church (as we will see later in this chapter), but it was not until the 12th century that the church passed a decree forbidding priests from marrying, and this was done to prevent a priest's assets being passed on to his dependents upon his death. All of his assets were to go to the church.

## The Crusades

Jerusalem holds great religious significance for Christians, Muslims, and Jews, and therefore control of the city has been a priority for all three groups. As a result, Jerusalem has been destroyed twice, attacked 52 times, and captured and recaptured 44 times.

Jerusalem has been the spiritual center of the Jewish people since 1000 BCE when King David established it as the capital of Israel. It is believed that King Solomon built the first Temple there around 960 BCE.

Jerusalem holds significance for Christians since they believe that Jesus was born in nearby Bethlehem and spent most of his life in Jerusalem. His crucifixion allegedly took place on Calvary Hill, also in Jerusalem. Constantine ordered the Church of the Holy Sepulchre to be built over the alleged location of Christ's tomb.

Islam regards Jerusalem as its third-holiest city. Muslims believe that Muhammad spent time in Jerusalem and it was from here that he ascended to heaven. They built the Dome of the Rock on the spot where Muhammad was said to have sat and prayed, which happens to be the exact same spot on the Temple Mount where King Solomon's Temple was built. The Al Aqsa Mosque is built on the southern side of the Temple Mount facing toward Mecca.

In 1076, the Muslims captured Jerusalem and over the next 200 years Christians fought to get it back. The Crusades were a series of military campaigns that took place between 1095 and 1291. Pope Gregory VII claimed to have struggled with reservations about the doctrinal validity of a holy war and the shedding of blood for the Lord, but resolved the question in favor of justified violence and ordered the first campaign in 1095. Invading crusaders destroyed and looted everything in their path and hundreds of thousands of people were killed.

Other campaigns in Spain and Eastern Europe

continued into the 15th century with the goal of eradicating both Muslims and Jews.

## Anti-Semitism

Suggesting that Jesus was ordered to be crucified by Pontius Pilate, the Prefect of Judea, would not go over well in getting Roman support for the new religion. However, by making it appear that the Jews had insisted on his death, and that Pilate had been reluctant, was a convenient way of relieving Roman sentiments and putting the blame on the Jews (a group that the Romans had been having problems with).

The story of Judas' betrayal of Jesus is another example of blaming the Jews. The name Judas is the Greek spelling for Judah, the name of the Jewish nation. Many scholars believe that the scenes involving Jesus and Judas, and Jesus and Pontius Pilate were inserted to show that Jesus was not a threat to Roman authority, making it easier for the Roman government to accept the new religion.

By blaming the Jews for Jesus' death set the stage for 2000 years of anti-Semitism culminating with the Holocaust of WW2. Jews became the scapegoats for all the problems of the world, and stories circulated claiming that Jews killed and ate Christian children during cannibalistic rituals.

By the year 380 CE Judaism was the only other legally accepted religion, but Jews were isolated as much as possible. Marriage between Jews and Christians was forbidden and ultimately the penalty for such intermarriage was execution for the woman.

## Slavery and racism justified in the Bible

Slavery was common in ancient times, and was condoned in the Bible. The Old Testament clearly sets out the humane working conditions under which slaves were to be kept (see Exodus chapter 21 and Leviticus chapter 25 among others). In Deuteronomy 20:10-16 we see that it was acceptable to obtain slaves through warfare.

In 1 Timothy 1:10 slave traders are condemned, and yet in numerous other places in the New Testament slaves are warned not to rebel, but to obey their masters.

Interestingly, in Deuteronomy 23:15 it states that you must not return runaway slaves to their masters, and yet in Philemon 1:1-25 Paul writes that he is returning Onesimus, a fugitive slave, back to his master Philemon. In this letter Paul suggests, but does not demand, that since Christ has freed Philemon then perhaps Philemon should free Onesimus. Paul's vagueness in this matter provided the early Church Fathers with the justification for their decision not to officially denounce slavery.

To be fair, it must be pointed out that not all Christians supported slavery. In 1435 Pope Eugene IV demanded the excommunication of all those engaged in the slave trade, and again in 1537 Pope Paul III condemned slavery. As well, since the early days of Christianity many priests and other church leaders actively worked against slavery. In the United States, as early as 1688, congregations of the Religious Society of Friends (Quakers) actively protested slavery. The Quaker's "Testimony of Equality" (their belief that all people are created equal in the eyes of God) was an important factor influencing the early abolitionist movement.

## The curse of Ham

Much of the justification for slavery and racism in Christianity comes from the Genesis story about the curse of Ham in Genesis 9:20-27.

This story takes place after the flood. Noah plants a vineyard and begins making wine, one day he has too much to drink and passes out naked. His son Ham discovers him in this condition and tells his brothers who go in and cover him up. When Noah wakes up he places a curse on Ham and his son Canaan and their descendents, making them the servants of Ham's brothers.

This seems like an excessive punishment for simply finding his father passed out naked, but many researchers have suggested that "seeing his nakedness" was a euphemism for having sexual relations, or possibly even anal penetration and that it was more likely that the grandson Canaan was the perpetrator.

The word Ham is very similar to the Hebrew and Egyptian words for black, and many Christians throughout history, including the founding father Origen, have claimed that Ham represents all black people, that Noah's curse caused their dark skin color.

This has been the justification for condemning dark skinned races to slavery as a punishment for Ham or Canaan's actions, and based on this story, the racist belief developed that black people had souls as black as their skin, thereby justifying whatever was done to them.

## Spreading the one Divine truth

As European explorers spread out throughout the world, in addition to their search for riches, a large part of the motivation for funding these expeditions was to convert the heathens to Christianity. Therefore, massacring and enslaving the darker skinned native populations was perfectly acceptable as long as they had first been given the opportunity for everlasting life by being exposed to Christianity.

## The Inquisition

An Inquisition was an ecclesiastical tribunal set up by the Roman Catholic Church ostensibly for the purpose of combating or suppressing heresy, but it also effectively controlled the general public through fear, while proving profitable for both the Church and the inquisitors through bribery and the seizure of personal property. In the early days the questioning and the penalties were relatively benign; however in 1245 Pope Innocent IV granted the Inquisitors and their assistants complete absolution for any acts of violence, and in 1252 he authorized the use of torture for the purposes of investigating and stamping out heresy (incredibly, this was not revoked until 1917).

Legally the Inquisition only had jurisdiction over baptized members of the Church, but effectively this encompassed most of the population since when the ruler converted his subjects were generally forced to convert. Non-Christians could still be tried for blasphemy in secular courts which were controlled by the Church.

There were four distinct periods of the Inquisition:

- the Medieval Inquisition (1184 - 1230)
- the Spanish Inquisition (1478 - 1834)
- the Portuguese Inquisition (1536 - 1821)
- the Roman Inquisition (1542 - 1860)

## The Medieval Inquisition

The earliest of the Inquisitions took place in southern France, southern Germany, and northern Italy. The goal was to stamp out heretic movements like the Waldensians, the Cathars, the Knights Templar, and the Beguines.

The **Waldensians** were in southern Germany and northern Italy, and this movement developed in part in response to church corruption. In particular, they were opposed to the veneration, bordering on worship, of saints, and the selling of artifacts and indulgences (in effect, get out of hell cards).

The **Cathars** in southern France were also opposed to church corruption, in particular the church's acquisition of massive wealth. They believed in the duality of God, that the evil God created the materialistic world and the good God created the spiritual world. They preached poverty, chastity, and modesty as a means of detaching themselves from materialism.

The **Beguines** were a women's mystic movement that had previously been recognized by the Church. Why they fell into disfavor is not certain, but it is suspected that the church was looking for new heresies to fight against and new sources of revenue to seize, so, at the Council of Vienne in the fourteenth century, they were proclaimed heretics and persecuted, with large numbers of them being burned at the stake in France.

The **Knights Templar** was founded as a military arm of the church during the crusades. They became a favored charity and grew rapidly in membership and power. They developed a large economic infrastructure and became very wealthy by developing an early form of international banking. It is believed that action against the Templars was initiated because the church became afraid of its growing power, and the King of France, Philip the Fair, wanted to seize their wealth.

## The Spanish Inquisition

The Spanish Inquisition was set up under the royal authority of King Ferdinand II in 1478. It operated in all Spanish colonies and territories and its initial goal was to rid the colonies of Jews and Muslims who had remained in Spain after Islamic control of Spain ended. Those Jews and Muslims who remained had "converted" to Catholicism under threat of death. Later, after the Reformation, the Spanish Inquisition went after Protestants as well. The Inquisition in Spain continued to operate until 1834, while in North America it continued until the Mexican War of Independence ended in 1821.

It is difficult to accurately assess exactly how many people were tried during the 350 year reign of terror that was the Spanish Inquisition, but it is estimated that more than 340,000 cases were tried and 3,000 and 5,000 of those cases resulted in execution.

## The Portuguese Inquisition

The Portuguese Inquisition began in 1536, and targeted the Sephardic Jews who had fled from Spain in 1492. It expanded into the Portuguese colonies of Brazil and Goa (on the west coast of India). The Goa Inquisition targeted Hindus and Muslims in addition to its initial target of Jews.

It is estimated that more than 30,000 cases were tried during the Portuguese Inquisition and more than 1,200 were executed.

## The Roman Inquisition

Pope Paul III established the "Congregation of the Holy Office of the Inquisition" in Rome in 1542. Staffed with cardinals and other church officials, it was given the task of maintaining and defending the faith.

In 1908 the name was changed to "The Sacred Congregation of the Holy Office", and then in 1965 the name was changed to its present name "Congregation for the Doctrine of the Faith", but regardless of the change of name, it is still the department in the Roman Catholic Church whose function is to suppress anything that does not support official Catholic doctrine. As I pointed out earlier, papal approval of the use of torture to extract a confession was only revoked in 1917.

## Famous cases

The most famous case tried by the Roman Inquisition was that of Italian physicist, mathematician, and astronomer

Galileo Galilei who, in 1633, was charged with heresy because he had the nerve to dispute church doctrine by stating that the earth and the other planets rotated around the sun.

Galileo was convicted and initially imprisoned but his sentence was later commuted to house arrest where he remained until his death in 1642. Publication of any of his works was banned by the church. Because of his "crime" he was refused burial in the Basilica of Santa Croce, next to the tombs of his father and other ancestors. Finally, on October 31, 1992, Pope John Paul II issued an official declaration acknowledging the church's error in its handling of the Galileo affair.

A more recent case took place in 1858 in Bologna, Italy and was instrumental in stirring up public opinion and ending the Roman Inquisition. Whether the Roman Inquisition ended at this point or simply changed tactics is a matter for discussion. What happened was that Inquisition agents kidnapped a 6-year-old Jewish boy, Edgardo Mortara, because they learned that the child had been secretly baptized as a baby by his Catholic nursemaid. Pope Pius IX justified the kidnapping because according to Papal law it was illegal for baptized Christians to be raised by Jews, and so he raised the boy as a Catholic in Rome while the boy's father spent years seeking international help to try to reclaim his son.

For more about this reprehensible (but unfortunately not unique) incident in church history read *"The Kidnapping of Edgardo Mortara"* by David Kertzer, ISBN 978-0679768173

## Offences and Penalties

So, what sorts of things could bring you to the attention of the Inquisitors?

The primary offenses were heresy, which means to hold an opinion that contradicts established religious teachings and blasphemy, which means showing disrespect for God, the Church, or sacred things. But these were not the only things that could get you into trouble, you could be charged with Judaizing which means associating with Jews or participating in Jewish rituals. You could also be charged with crimes involving immorality such as bigamy, sodomy (meaning homosexuality), adultery, or bestiality.

Finally, you could be charged with divination, witchcraft, or sorcery which I will discuss in more detail later in this chapter.

If you went before the Inquisition it was very unlikely that you would be found innocent since you would probably be tortured until they extracted a confession. But it was possible that the trial could be suspended, and you could go free with the threat hanging over you that the process could be continued at any time. A suspended trial was effectively an acquittal without stating that you had been wrongly charged.

You were more likely to be condemned to death if you were wealthy, since the Inquisitor would be entitled to seize your assets. If it was deemed that your crime did not warrant the death penalty you could be fined and publicly whipped. The poor could do penances for their crimes, in which case you would have to publicly confess your crime and renounce it, and part of the punishment would include public humiliation. The humiliation could include being paraded through town wearing a special penitential garment (called a Sanbenito during the Spanish Inquisition).

If you were a poor, but healthy male you could be sentenced to the galley ships as an oarsman. Being a galley slave was effectively a death sentence since the living conditions were very unhealthy and most died within a few years.

If you were sentenced to death the actual execution would be turned over to the secular authorities since, hypocritically, the church leaders did not want to do the actual execution. The execution involved a public burning at the stake. If you repented you could be shown mercy and garroted (strangled) before being burnt, otherwise you would be burnt alive.

## Martin Luther and the Reformation

In the 15th and 16th centuries a movement sprung up in western Europe demanding reform in the Catholic Church. Basically this group opposed what they believed to be false doctrines and corruption in the church. Among the issues that most concerned them were the sale of indulgences, this was where you could pay the church to have your sins forgiven (get out of hell cards) and corruption in the clergy, specifically the practice of simony (buying and selling of clerical offices).

On October 31, 1517 Martin Luther, a German priest and professor of theology, posted a letter on the door of the Church of All Saints in Wittenberg Germany. This letter, which has come to be known as the *"Ninety-Five*

*Theses,"* marked the start of the Protestant Reformation which ultimately split the church in two.

The printing press had recently been invented and so these *"Ninety-Five Theses"* were quickly translated from Latin into German, and printed and distributed throughout Europe.

Martin Luther refused to recant what he had written and he was excommunicated by Pope Leo X on January 3, 1521. On May 25, 1521 Emperor Charles V banned Luther's writings and ordered his arrest. The Emperor's order made it a crime for anyone in Germany to give Luther food or shelter and made it legal for anyone to kill him.

It sounds like he was a good man standing up for his principles against a corrupt bureaucracy. Well, yes but . . . as time went on the reformers sincerity and zeal in rooting out evil ushered in a period of unprecedented suffering for many people.

## Martin Luther and Nazi Anti-Semitism

After the Reformation, in the early days of the Lutheran Church, Martin Luther attempted to convert Jews to Protestant Christianity but when he was unsuccessful he turned on them. He wrote the book *"On the Jews and Their Lies"* in 1543 in which he called them venomous beasts, vipers, and disgusting scum who should be lodged in stables, and advocated the destruction of synagogues and the annihilation of the Jewish people.

The Nazis used Martin Luther's book as moral

justification for their "final solution" to the Jewish problem during the Second World War.

Here is a quote from Martin Luther's book *"On the Jews and Their Lies"* that pretty much sums up his thoughts regarding Jews:

> *"If I had to baptize a Jew, I would take him to the bridge of the Elbe, hang a stone around his neck and push him over with the words 'I baptize thee in the name of Abraham'."*

It is true that modern day Lutheran Churches have since disassociated themselves from Luther's anti-Semitic statements, but still, the damage is done.

## The body is evil

The belief that the body was evil resulted in washing being seen as a vice to be discouraged. When hygiene deteriorated disease became rampant, and towns were decimated by epidemics. The plague in the 6th century decimated the Roman Empire and strengthened the church's control over medical treatment. The field of medical research was considered heresy; disease was a punishment from God for refusing to submit to the church's authority, and was to be accepted stoically. Wise women, herbalist healers, were discredited, and as we will discuss later, called witches.

By the time of the Reformation, the only church sanctioned physicians were men, and their primary form of treatment was bloodletting. "Bleeding" a patient to improve health was based on the role of menstruation in women. As far back as Hippocrates it was believed that menstruation functioned to purify the body. Later on, as the Christian era progressed, it was believed that menstruation was a symbol of God's punishment of women so, by the middle ages, bleeding became a way of "mortifying the flesh," a punishment for whatever sin had caused the disease. It was believed that bleeding would prevent toxic imbalances, as well as prevent sexual desire. By the 17th century this practice killed thousands, if not tens of thousands, of people every year.

## Sex is evil

The enjoyment of sex was proof that Adam's original sin was passed down from mother to child in the womb. Sex should be avoided except for purposes of procreation. Women were seen as being responsible for sin by causing men to lust (an argument still used throughout the world to this day).

Followers of the Protestant Reformation movement were warned that it was sinful to enjoy sex even with one's own spouse.

## The Puritans

Puritans were a particularly zealous splinter group of Protestants who thought that the English Reformation had not gone far enough. They advocated greater personal and group piety, one aspect of which was their insistence on a strict keeping of the Christian sabbath. In England it was the custom that Sunday morning was devoted to church while in the afternoon the public enjoyed sporting events. The Puritans objected to this practice believing that playing games on the sabbath constituted a violation of God's law and demanded that sporting events be banned on the sabbath. When they were unsuccessful in having their religious views made into law they began migrating to the New England colonies, not in search of religious freedom as we have always been taught, but looking for a new land where they could enforce their own brand of religious extremism.

For Puritans, pleasure of any sort was evil, and even celebrating holidays was banned. On Sundays in 17th century New England it was illegal to take a walk, go swimming, go sledding, or even be caught laughing. Offenders would be brought before the local magistrate for sentencing which could include public humiliation by being placed in stocks which were heavy wooden frames with holes that held the prisoner's ankles and wrists. The pillory was similar, but was designed so the person held in it would be in a standing position with the offender's head and wrists secured and was primarily used for people of a higher social standing. While in the stocks they would be subjected to verbal abuse and have rotten food thrown at them from passersby.

They could also be forced to wear a large letter on their clothing, the letter referring to the crime committed. Sometimes, instead of just wearing a letter, the letter was branded onto their forehead or other body part with a heated branding iron.

A person who had the nerve to speak out against the religion could have their tongue pierced with a hot spike. Few people were foolish enough to speak out.

## The ducking stool

The ducking (or cucking) stool was a form of punishment that the Puritans brought with them from Europe. It was a form of torture similar to modern day "waterboarding." It was used on women who argued with their husbands. The woman would be tied to a chair or stool which was attached to a long teeter-totter like arm or lever. The woman would be repeatedly dunked in a body of water for the number of times that the judge demanded.

## Treatment of Women in Christianity

In the pagan religions and in early Gnostic Christianity it was understood that God had both male and female aspects, but later when they made God male it was only logical that male supremacy was an extension of heavenly order.

In 1 Cor. 11:8-9 Paul attempts to explain the reason for male supremacy, *"For the man is not of the woman: but the woman of the man. Neither was the man created for the woman; but the woman for the man."*

1 Timothy 2:11-13 *"Let the woman learn in silence with all subjection. But I suffer not a woman to teach, nor to usurp authority over the man, but to be in silence. For Adam was first formed, then Eve."*

As was mentioned earlier in this book, when the mathematician and philosopher Hypatia was dragged from her chariot and murdered by Christian monks in 415 on her way to give a lecture at the University of Alexandria, Bishop Cyril (later to be Saint Cyril) explained that she was murdered because she was a woman who went against God's commandments by presuming to teach men.

## The witch hunts

Societies always seem to need someone to blame for their problems. Rather than looking inside ourselves for what is causing a particular situation we prefer to blame others. Just as the Jews were blamed for the economic problems during pre-war Germany, and illegal Mexican immigration in Arizona is being blamed for the US drug problem as well as the economic and social problems today, independent and intelligent women were convenient scapegoats for every conceivable social ill in the 16th and 17th centuries.

As bad as the various Inquisitions were in Catholic countries, the Protestant Reformation unleashed a reign of terror in Europe never before seen. Far more women were accused of witchcraft and executed in Protestant countries than in Catholic countries under the Inquisition.

Prior to the Reformation small numbers of people were tried for sorcery and witchcraft but after the Reformation the trials took on a new zeal.

The numbers are difficult to verify, but researchers have concluded that perhaps two hundred women were burned at the stake as witches in Catholic countries under the Inquisition, while the followers of Martin Luther ordered the torture and execution of as many as seven million women suspected of being witches during the sixteenth and seventeenth centuries.

## Martin Luther and women

Martin Luther was a misogynist. He, like most of the church fathers before him, believed that women were responsible for original sin. Here are some of his thoughts regarding women:

> "God created Adam master and lord of living creatures, but Eve spoilt all, when she persuaded him to set himself above God's will. Tis you women, with your tricks and artifices, that lead men into error."

> "No gown worse becomes a woman than the desire to be wise."

> "The word and works of God is quite clear, that women were made either to be wives or prostitutes."

> "Men have broad and large chests, and small narrow hips, and more understanding than women, who have but small and narrow breasts, and broad hips, to the end they should remain at home, sit still, keep house, and bear and bring up children."

> "Even though they grow weary and wear themselves out with child-bearing, it does not matter; let them go on bearing children till they die, that is what they are there for."

## Martin Luther and superstition

Almost all Christians of this time period were strong believers in demonic forces. Martin Luther was no exception.

Here are some of Martin Luther's beliefs about demons and witchcraft which helped fuel the witch hysteria.

*"When I was a child there were many witches, and they bewitched both cattle and men, especially children."*

*"The Devil can so completely assume the human form, when he wants to deceive us, that we may well lie with what seems to be a woman, of real flesh and blood, and yet all the while 'tis only the Devil in the shape of a woman. Tis the same with women, who may think that a man is in bed with them, yet 'tis only the Devil; and... the result of this connection is oftentimes an imp of darkness, half mortal, half devil...."*

*"A large number of deaf, crippled and blind people are afflicted solely through the malice of the demon. And one must in no wise doubt that plagues, fevers and every sort of evil come from him."*

*"As for the demented, I hold it certain that all beings deprived of reason are thus afflicted only by the Devil."*

*"Idiots, the lame, the blind, the dumb, are men in whom the devils have established themselves: and all the physicians who heal these infirmities, as though they proceeded from natural causes, are ignorant blockheads...."*

*"Our bodies are always exposed to Satan. The maladies I suffer are not natural, but Devil's spells."*

*"The Devil, too, sometimes steals human children; it is not infrequent for him to carry away infants within*

*the first six weeks after birth, and to substitute in their place imps...."*

The general view was that the world was the realm of the devil, and mental illness was a result of demonic possession.

After the Reformation it was sinful to believe in help from saints or magic. In their eagerness to distance themselves from the Catholic Church the leaders of the Reformation vehemently opposed any form of veneration of saints or of the Virgin Mary. Anything resembling the sacred feminine of the old pagan religions was distorted to make it less appealing. For example, originally the image of the crone, an old woman, was synonymous with wisdom and benevolent healing, but over time it came to symbolize witchcraft and evil

Since physical illness was a punishment for spiritual failings, the church was opposed to any attempt to improve the course of one's life, teaching that one should be content to suffer whatever God inflicted on you.

Therefore, anyone with a knowledge of herbs or healing was considered a witch. Midwives, or anyone who relieved the suffering of childbirth, were considered witches since they were interfering with God's punishment of women.

Once accused of witchcraft it was virtually impossible to escape. The accused either died during the torture and were therefore deemed to be innocent, or if they lived they were found guilty and died by being burnt at the stake.

I don't think for the purposes of this book it is necessary

for me to go into detail about the methods of torture used. There are many other books and reference materials that discuss this in detail. I think it suffices to say that this period of history illustrated mankind's incredible capacity for creative depravity.

Obviously, in this chapter I have barely scratched the surface of this disturbing topic, but hopefully this information has opened your eyes to the dark side of Christianity. If you are interested in learning more I highly recommend that you start with the book *"The Dark Side of Christian History"* by Helen Ellerbe ISBN 978-0-9644873-4-5.

# 13

## Pagan Saviors

Long before the birth of the Jesus Christ that we have been taught about since Sunday school there were numerous stories about saviors who were sent from God to save mankind. Some researchers claim there are at least 50 such saviors who predate the carpenter from Nazareth, and whose stories contain many similarities.

### Miraculous births

The ancients obviously believed that a savior, a son of God, should have a purer and holier origin than the rest of us mortals and so stories of miraculous births were one of the first evidences of divine status.

We are all familiar with the story of Jesus' birth, how a young virgin named Mary conceived a child from the Holy Spirit, and ended up giving birth to him in a stable. But you might be surprised to know that this story is not unique.

It is claimed that the mother of the Persian prophet and philosopher Zoroaster was impregnated by a ray of divine light sometime around 1100 BCE.

The virgin Alcmene claimed that the god Zeus was the father of her son, the Divine Redeemer Alcides or Hercules about 1280 BCE.

It is claimed that Mayence, the mother of Hesus of the Druids, was a virgin when she was impregnated by god more than 2000 years BCE.

Pythais, the mother of Pythagoras (the Greek philosopher and founder of the religious movement Pythagoreanism) was apparently a virgin when she was impregnated by the god Apollo in 570 BCE. Of course other biographers claim that Pythagoras was the son of a merchant named Mnesarchus.

Although not a virgin birth (his mother had 7 previous children who were all killed) Lord Krishna was also born without sexual union, by "mental transmission" from the mind of his father into the womb of his mother about 1200 BCE.

In some stories, the ancient Roman goddess Juno, the mother of the Greek god Mars was impregnated as a result of touching the petals of a flower, and then later conceived the god Vulcan by being overcome by a gust of divine wind.

The Chinese monarch, Yu the Great, the legendary founder of the Xia Dynasty was apparently conceived when his mother was struck by a star while travelling. However other stories claim that he was he was born from the corpse of his father.

In my opinion though, the ancient Egyptian god Horus had the most miraculous birth. After Horus' father, the god Osiris, was murdered, his widow, the goddess Isis, retrieved all of Osiris' dismembered body parts, (except for his penis which had been thrown into the Nile River and was eaten by a catfish) and used her magic powers to resurrect him and create a gold phallus which she used to conceive her son Horus.

## The savior's birth is announced by stars

We have all heard how there was a star over the stable in Bethlehem that led the wise men to Jesus, but did you realize that many previous "saviors" such as Yu the Great, Pythagoras, and Lord Krishna also had miraculous stars in their stories.

## Angels and wise men visit the savior

Like the story of Jesus, the new born Confucius (551 BCE), and Lord Krishna (1200 BCE), Pythagoras (570 BCE), Mithra (1100 BCE), and Zoroaster (1100 BCE) were also visited by angels and wise men.

## A most auspicious birthday

By a most amazing coincidence, Bacchus, Adonis, Krishna, Sakia, and Mithra (among others) were all born on December 25.

## Royal bloodlines, but humble conditions

Many of the saviors prior to Jesus were descended from royalty, but in order to teach the world about humility they were born in humble circumstances. For example, Lord

Krishna, the Hindu deity and eighth reincarnation of the god Vishnu the Supreme Being was born in a cave. He is often depicted as a young man playing a flute, accompanied by cows, emphasizing his position as the divine herdsman.

## Their lives were endangered from birth

In the story of Jesus, we are told that King Herod was so afraid of eventually being overthrown by Jesus that he tried to have him killed by ordering the death of all children under the age of two.

Similarly, Krishna's life was in danger because his uncle, the king, wanted him killed and ordered all children under the age of two killed. His uncle was afraid of a prophecy that predicted that he would die at the hands of his sister's eighth son. So shortly after his birth Krishna was hidden and raised by foster parents. Throughout his life he avoided numerous assassination attempts.

In the story of Horus (2400 BCE), when Isis became pregnant she fled to the marshlands of Egypt to hide from her brother Set who wanted to kill her son.

The mother of Hercules/Alcides was also forced to go into hiding to save her infant child's life.

## Crucified to save mankind

Every Christian "knows" that Jesus was crucified to atone for the sins of mankind, and that he rose from the grave after 3 days and ascended to heaven.

But according to Kersey Graves in his book *"The*

*World's Sixteen Crucified Saviors,"* there were at least fifteen religious myths that preceded the story of Jesus which involve the crucifixion of sin-atoning gods. Some of the gods he lists I have not been able to verify, which is not surprising since the Christian church made a serious effort to destroy all records of other earlier religions, but the following can definitely be verified:

## Horus (2400 BCE)

It is claimed that Horus was crucified along with two thieves and was buried in a tomb, only to be resurrected 3 days later.

## Krishna (1200 BCE)

There are illustrations dating from approximately 1200 BCE which show Krishna being crucified, nailed to a cross similar to the later description of Jesus' crucifixion.

## Tammuz of Syria (1160 BCE)

The god Tammuz was a Sumerian shepherd-god, an annual life-death-rebirth deity whose crucifixion story included his descent into the underworld (hell) to secure his wife's release. The Babylonians mourned his death every year at the summer solstice.

## Quetzalcoatl of Mexico (900 BCE)

Quetzalcoatl was the feathered serpent creator deity worshipped by the Aztecs in Mexico. Like most gods, his was a virgin birth. He was a twin, he and his brother together made up one of three gods, a mediator between earth and sky (the heavens). He is credited with recreating mankind for the fifth time after the first four groups of people had been destroyed. He allegedly went down to the underworld and created mankind from the bones of the previous people using blood from a wound in his penis.

In one version of his story he burns himself to death out of remorse for having seduced his sister, while another version is that he flew up into the heavens and was crucified in the sky to prevent mankind from being destroyed again.

## Esus (or Hesus) of the Celtic Druids, (834 BCE)

Esus was one of three Celtic gods, a trinity similar to the concept of God the Father, God the Son, and God the Holy Ghost in Christian doctrine. I could not find any verifiable references to ancient illustrations of Esus being crucified himself, but modern Neo-Druids depict Esus as having been crucified with a lamb on one side and an elephant on the other. However, there are ancient illustrations of human victims being tied to a tree and whipped to death as sacrifices to Esus.

## Sakia of India (600 BCE)

In most Buddhist traditions, the enlightened one Siddhartha Gautama died at the age of 80 after eating a poisonous meal, but there is another version in which he is a Hindu god called Sakia and was executed for the crime of picking a flower in a garden, and was killed by an arrow which was shot through his body and pinned him to a tree. As in the Jesus story, the savior was killed and ascended to heaven and took with him the sins of his followers.

## Was the Egyptian god Horus the model for the life story of Jesus?

Many researchers, including Tom Harpur in his book *"The Pagan Christ,"* point out that there are a number of similarities between the story of Horus and that of Jesus 2400 years later that it would seem that the writer's of the New Testament were influenced by the earlier Eqyptian stories.

1) Sirius, the morning star announced the birth of Horus.

2) His mother Isis was forced to flee into the wilderness to save the life of her newborn son.

3) There is no record of his life between the ages of twelve and thirty.

4) Horus was baptized in the River Eridanus by a man who was later beheaded.

5) Horus has disciples to whom he teaches a message of love and everlasting life.

6) Horus delivered a "sermon on a mountain."

7) He performs numerous miracles including walking on water, casting out demons, and healing the sick.

8) Horus is called "the lamb of God" and was crucified to atone for his followers' sins.

9) After his death he is resurrected 3 days later and descends into Hades to bring the dead up to heaven.

## Or, was the Hindu Lord Krishna the model for the life story of Jesus?

There are even more similarities between the story of Krishna and that of Jesus 1200 years later.

1) First, there is his miraculous birth in a cave, not a virgin birth, but without sexual union between his parents.

2) The infant was immediately recognized as being special and was visited by angels and wise men who were guided to him by a star.

3) His life was threatened by a ruler who ordered the death of all children under the age of two.

4) He and his parents miraculously escape from death by the parting of the River Jumna which allows them to cross on dry land (like Moses and the parting of the Red Sea).

5) He shows signs of greatness at an early age and then spends years alone in the desert meditating.

6) He is often portrayed herding cows.

7) Upon rejoining civilization he ceremonially bathes in the River Ganges before beginning to teach.

8) He has 12 disciples, one of whom (Arjoon) is his best friend.

9) He taught through the use of parables.

10) There is a story where he tells his disciples how to fish and they pull in a miraculous catch.

11) He performs numerous other miracles including healing the sick and raising people from the dead.

12) He teaches the same message of love and forgiveness that Jesus later taught.

13) Upon entering the city of Madura the crowds come out to greet him and carpet the ground with coconut palm branches.

14) He is anointed with oil by women followers.

15) He was crucified to atone for his followers' sins.

16) The world was thrown into darkness at the time of his crucifixion.

17) After his death he appears to his followers and tells them that he will always be with them.

I think that it is pretty obvious that the writers of the New Testament were influenced by the earlier Egyptian and Hindu stories.

# Some other gods that the Jesus story is modeled after

## Osiris - The Egyptian God who offered eternal life

Osiris was the Egyptian god of the underworld who granted all life. He is described as the "Lord of love", and it was believed that he would rise up from the dead and judge the dead in the afterlife. All those who were associated with him would achieve eternal life. A person was considered to be associated with Osiris through a series of death rituals.

## Bacchus (Roman)/Dionysus (Greek) - "Born again"

In Roman mythology Bacchus, and in Greek mythology Dionysus, was the god of wine and grapes. He inspired joyful worship, and ecstasy, and was known as the Liberator, who frees you from your normal life and brings an end to care and worry. Bacchus/Dionysus was also the god who controlled communication between the living and the dead. As a god of resurrection he wears a fox-skin which symbolizes new life.

As with most gods, Bacchus/Dionysus had a miraculous birth. In the Roman version of the story his mother was a mortal woman, Semele, who had an extramarital affair with the god Zeus. Zeus' wife found out about the affair while Semele was pregnant and to get revenge, she tricked Semele into demanding that Zeus reveal himself in all his glory as proof of his godhood. He agreed, and showed himself to her wreathed in bolts of lightning. Since mortals could not look upon an undisguised god without dying she perished, but Zeus rescued the unborn Bacchus by sewing him into his thigh. A few months later, Bacchus was born fully-grown from his father Zeus' thigh. Since he first grew in the body of his mother and then in the thigh of his father he was considered to be "twice-born" or "born again".

In the Greek version of the story Dionysus was the son of Zeus and Persephone (the queen of the underworld). Zeus' jealous wife attempted to kill the young child by sending other gods (Titans) to tear him to pieces. Zeus drove the attacking gods away with his thunderbolts, but only after they had eaten everything but Dionysus' heart. One version has Zeus using the heart to recreate Dionysus in the womb of his mother, while another version is that Zeus gave Semele the heart to eat to impregnate her, hence he was again "twice-born" or "born again".

This rebirth in both versions of the story is the main reason why Bacchus/Dionysus was revered in the secret "mystery" religions, upon which much of Christianity was based.

## Thor (son of Odin)

Thor was the god of the ancient Germanic/Norse peoples from at least 2000 BCE. Thor traveled in a chariot drawn by two goats, and on a famous fishing trip battled the evil Midgard Serpent and came close to killing it, but the serpent got away.

According to the legend, Thor will battle the great serpent again at the end of the world when the serpent comes out of the sea and poisons the sky. Thor will be successful in slaying the serpent but will die in the process of saving mankind.

# Who actually wrote the New Testament?

No one really knows for sure who wrote the any of the Bible since it is made up of 66 different books written by more than 39 authors over a period of at least 1,500 years. As to who wrote the Gospels, one thing is certain, they were not written by peers of Jesus. The earliest of them, the Gospel of Mark, was written no earlier than 70 CE.

For the first few hundred years of the Christian era there were hundreds of versions of the gospels. Bishop Irenaeus compiled the first list of biblical writings that in any way resemble our New Testament around 180 CE, years after any of the supposed peers of Jesus would have died. In 393 Bishop Athanasius had a list of approved versions ratified at the Council of Hippo, and ordered the burning of all unapproved versions. By destroying other versions, followers eventually got the impression that the approved versions were the only versions.

# Was Jesus a real person?

As you can see there are common threads throughout all of these stories. All religions claim that their savior was an actual person, and that the events they describe in their sacred literature were actual events, so does it still seem likely that Jesus of Nazareth was a real person and the stories we have heard about him actually took place? Or is it more likely that his story is another allegory created to teach about universal human concerns?

Personally, I am not convinced that the actual person really existed. My reasons are as follows:

1) There is no direct archeological evidence of his existence. As we saw earlier in this book, Jesus' tomb was conveniently "discovered" by Constantine's mother about 300 years after his death. She also discovered the actual cross he was crucified on which was in pristine condition in spite of being buried for 300 years, as well as his robes. The story of the soldiers casting lots for his robes was not added to the gospel story until after Helena "found" the robes.

2) The New Testament was written long after any eyewitnesses would have died. Paul never met Jesus.

3) The Romans kept very extensive records and yet there are no records of the trial or execution taking place, and there are no other ancient works that specifically mention Jesus.

4) If he did exist his name was not Jesus. The letter J did not exist in any language until the 16th century.

Certainly, if he did exist, most if not all of the stories attributed to him were clearly taken from earlier religious traditions.

*"What event of Christ's life, then, can be accepted as certain when no record was made of it until the time was forgotten, and none for at least half a century after the dawn of the Christian era, when nearly all who witnessed it must have been dead?"*

**Kersey Graves**
Spiritualist and author of
"The World's Sixteen Crucified Saviors"

# 14

## Is there a place for religion?

It seems that man has a burning desire for some form of religion, and wants to be told what to do. We all want some authority figure to confirm that we are on the right path, and by claiming to be divinely appointed to spread a divinely approved religion, the priesthood of all forms of worship have provided that assurance and in doing so have succeeded in deceiving and enslaving us.

### Fear, the foundation of religion

Religion is based primarily upon fear. It is the fear of the unknown, and the corresponding desire to have someone powerful to look out for you in times of trouble. Religious leaders throughout history have preyed on this universal fear of the unknown.

### Divine dictation?

We are told that the scriptures are the Divinely inspired word of God. Ignore the contradictions and the cruelty. Ignore the fact that they have been continually modified throughout the centuries to emphasize whatever doctrine the religious establishment chose to focus on at the time.

We are expected to believe that an all powerful being dictated the words to the writers and yet even with this "Divine dictation" the Bible has needed editing and revision for thousands of years. As the author of numerous books, I have a particularly hard time with this idea. While it is true that no author is ever totally satisfied with their writing, at some point you have to say "enough, I've made my point, it is time to move on." Surely after all these re-writes, wouldn't an all powerful god decide that it was good enough, or else start fresh with a new secretary?

## Worshipping a man who likely never existed

As I pointed out in the previous chapter, I think that there is plenty of evidence to suggest that the historical person, Jesus of Nazareth, did not exist. However, I am not suggesting that there is no value in the Christ story; on the contrary I think that by recognizing it as a story it allows you to begin to understand the universal lessons that all the savior stories throughout history teach. The problem occurs when people insist on taking the story literally and are adamant that their understanding is the only correct version. Recognizing the Christ story as an allegory takes away the fear of death and allows one the freedom to admit that there are some things that we just don't understand and can never know for certain. Admitting that you don't know everything is freeing.

## Atheism vs. Agnosticism

Atheism is the belief that there are no gods, that there is no higher power, while agnosticism is the view that the truth of any claims about the existence or non-existence of any god, or any other religious claim is unknowable. An agnostic may suspect that something is true and yet recognizes that many things are impossible to know for certain.

The English biologist, Thomas Henry Huxley, created the expression in 1860 but many philosophers have held agnostic positions throughout history. I think it is possible for a person to benefit from religion while maintaining the agnostic position that there are some things that we will never know for sure as long as we are alive, and since we can't know things for certain then there is no point in taking a tough stand and trying to convert others to your point of view.

## Freethinkers

Spiritualism, the religion that I am associated with, was started back in the mid 1800's by a group of "Freethinkers." Freethought is a philosophy that contends that opinions should be formed on the basis of logic and evidence and should not be influenced by authority or tradition. Basically, it is wrong for anyone to believe anything without sufficient evidence, or to demand that others adopt your position. The Freethinkers who started Spiritualism were liberals who espoused such radical ideals as racial, social, and sexual equality, and the abolition of slavery.

Spiritualism as a religion has fallen off dramatically since the height of its popularity in the 1870's when it was the fastest growing religion in the United States. I think this falling off is partly because of evidences of mediumistic fraud (or just mediocre mediumship), but also because it does not trade in fear. We believe in a higher power, a god of each person's own understanding, whatever that means for you, but there is no hell, and therefore no need of a savior to atone for us. So if there is nothing to fear, who cares if you go to church on Sunday, which as you can imagine, doesn't result in huge turnouts.

## Freethought in Buddhism

Buddhists practice something similar to the philosophy of freethought. They teach that it is acceptable to doubt, to question, and never to accept anything simply because of tradition. Instead, look into your own conscience, and investigate for yourself.

## What if there is no hell?

If there is no hell does that mean that we are free to do whatever we want? Well, yes but, if we want to live in harmony with others we have to observe certain universal ethical principles, most importantly, the golden rule of all religions which is to treat others the way you would want to be treated.

## As children we inherit our opinions

Generally, our religious beliefs depend on where we were born. If we were born in India to Hindu parents we would probably be Hindu, in Saudi Arabia to Muslim parents we would be Muslim, and in the North America or western Europe we would probably be Christian. We are molded by our surroundings.

Even Spiritualists are influenced by the western world's cultural leaning toward Christianity. We all carry with us remnants of those childhood influences, some to a greater degree than others, and so some so called "Christian Spiritualist" churches exist to make people who still carry the baggage of their Christian heritage feel comfortable. This doesn't suit me personally, but as long as they emphasize love and kindness for others and maintain a tolerance of religious diversity why should I care whether they occasionally mention Jesus?

## What do people get from religion?

Everyone wants a sense of belonging. Religions are no different from inner city youth gangs in this sense. We are social creatures who hate to walk alone. Being part of a group is reassuring, acceptance by the group means that people like us, we are important. Aside from the fear of death and hell, the greatest fear of most people is the threat of being ostracized by their peer group.

Religious beliefs are emotional, not rational. People cannot be swayed from their religious beliefs by logic. So, most people will not give up their religious beliefs regardless of compelling evidence against them. This is something that I thought about a lot as I wrote this book, was I wasting my time writing a book that most religious people would never read, was I in effect "preaching to the choir" writing a book that only people who already know this information would be willing to read?

## All religions are essentially the same

Religions are all based on a belief in a supernatural power that man can influence through worship and prayer. This makes us feel in control in a world that often seems out of control.

What the supernatural power is, and what form the worship takes are really only superficial differences. Even medical science is a form of religion, doctors are the high priests, study is a form of worship for the priests, prescription drugs are the sacraments, and obedience is expected from the followers.

There is nothing wrong with wanting a sense of power and control for ourselves, as long as we do not then use that feeling of power to attempt to control others.

## Everyone wants the same things

All human beings are the same. We all want to live a comfortable life. We all want loving relationships. We all want our children to be healthy and happy and enjoy the promise of a bright future. We want to feel in control of our lives. We want to be part of a group.

There can never be peace on earth until we stop taking religious teachings literally

As long as we continue to believe that our religion is the one true religion, as long as we believe that "god" is on our side in any dispute, and that we have an obligation to spread our particular dogma we can never have peace. History has shown us over and over again the almost unfathomable evil that results when we use our religious beliefs to persecute and ostracize those who hold different beliefs.

But once we recognize that all religions, instead of being of Divine authenticity, are purely and entirely of human origin we can begin to benefit from the universal "truths" of all religious myths.

I hope that what you have read in this book has begun to make you think about all the "truths" about religion, Christianity, and God that you have been taught with a more questioning mind. But don't take my word for it, be a modern day "Freethinker" and research it for yourself. In the next chapter I have compiled a list of books to get you started.

*"The Devil has taught to the Aztecs the same things which God has taught to Christendom."*

**Hernando Cortez,** (1485-1547)
Spanish Conquistador who led the
Conquest of Mexico 1519-1521

# Recommended Reading

15

If you would like to read more about this fascinating topic here are some books that I highly recommend.

## The Pagan Christ: Is Blind Faith Killing Christianity
by Tom Harpur
ISBN 978-0-8027-7741-6

I wish that everyone would read this book. The author, Tom Harpur, is a retired Anglican priest and professor of Greek and New Testament at the University of Toronto. His book explains how, after years of study, he finally concluded that the historical Jesus did not exist. He explains how, long before the arrival of Jesus Christ, ancient people believed in the coming of a messiah, of a virgin birth, and a Madonna and her child, and what had begun as a universal belief system built on myth and allegory was transformed, by the third and fourth centuries CE, into a religion based on the literal interpretation of myths and symbols. Harpur proposes that, in spite of the Jesus story not being actual literal history, religion still has an important spiritual meaning and purpose.

## The World's Sixteen Crucified Saviors
by Kersey Graves
ISBN 978-1-60206-280-1

The author Kersey Graves (1813-1883) was a Spiritualist and "Freethinker." In this book he breaks the Christ myth down into its component parts and shows how the story of Jesus has its roots in earlier folklore.

## The Christ Conspiracy: The Greatest Story Ever Sold
by Acharya S
ISBN 978-09328137-4-9

This book presents evidence that shows that Christianity and the story of Jesus Christ were deliberately created in order to unify the Roman Empire under one state religion. This book shows how the founders of Christianity drew from religious myths that existed long before the Christian era and reworked them into the story known to us today as the Bible. The author claims that there was no actual person named Jesus, that the story of Jesus was created by combining the stories of earlier deities such as Mithras, Hercules, and Dionysus.

## The Dark Side of Christian History
by Helen Ellerbe
ISBN 0-9644873-4-9

This fascinating and easy to read book shows how, over the last two thousand years, the Christian Church has oppressed and brutalized millions of individuals. It covers the church's persecution of heretics, its burning of libraries, the Crusades, the Inquisition, and the witch-hunts. The author shows how the church has left a legacy which fosters sexism, racism, intolerance, and the desecration of the natural environment.

## Pagan Origins of the Christ Myth
by John G. Jackson
ISBN 978-0-910309-53-0

This is a short booklet (36 pages) that was originally published in 1941. It explains how religion, and the myth about the fall of man in particular, is based on man's yearning for immortality. It goes on to discuss some of the early savior myths.

## Bible Myths and Their Parallels in Other Religions
by Thomas William Doane
ISBN 978-11506530-1-8

Originally published in 1882, this book shows how Christianity has parallels in all the ancient systems of worship.

## The Two Babylons
by Alexander Hislop
ISBN 978-16042448-6-1

Originally published in 1916, this book explains how many traditions of Roman Catholicism in fact don't come from

Christ's teachings but from an ancient Babylonian "Mystery" religion that was centered on Nimrod, his wife Semiramis, and a child Tammuz. You will discover how practices like confession, and crossing ones self originated with that earlier religion.

**The Jesus Mysteries: Was the "Original Jesus" a Pagan God?**
by Timothy Freke and Peter Gandy
ISBN 978-0609807989

In this book the authors explain how the story of Jesus was adapted from the symbolism of the ancient Osiris-Dionysus myths, and that the early Christian church attempted to destroy the evidence of the connection between Christianity and the pagan mysteries.

**101 Myths of the Bible: How Ancient Scribes Invented Biblical History**
by Gary Greenberg
ISBN 978-1570718427

This is a fascinating book about the Egyptian myths and ancient folklore behind the Old Testament legends. In it the author claims that:

-King David's bodyguard, not David, killed Goliath
-Noah's Ark did not land on Mount Ararat
-Samson did not pull down a Philistine temple
-There are at least two versions of the Ten Commandments
-The walls of Jericho were destroyed 300 years before Joshua got there

-Sodom and Gomorrah were mythical cities that never existed

## Who Wrote the New Testament?: The Making of the Christian Myth
by Burton L. Mack
ISBN 978-00606551-8-1

This book explains how the four Gospels are fictional mythologies created by different groups for various purposes.

## Christianity Before Christ by John G. Jackson ISBN 978-0910309202

This book explains that there is nothing new or original in Christianity, that all its components were well developed in earlier cultures that flourished long before the time Christ is alleged to have lived.

*"There are many things which are true which it is not useful for the vulgar crowd to know; and certain things which although they are false it is expedient for the people to believe otherwise."*

**St. Augustine, 354-430 CE**
Bishop of Hippo Regius,
one of the most important figures in the
development of Christianity

# 16

## "Why I Am an Agnostic"

**The following is an excerpt from a speech entitled "Why I Am an Agnostic" by Robert Green Ingersoll originally published in 1896. In a few pages he sums up much of the information in this book.**

I have concluded that all religions had the same foundation -- a belief in the supernatural -- a power above nature that man could influence by worship -- by sacrifice and prayer.

I found that all religions rested on a mistaken conception of nature -- that the religion of a people was the science of that people, that is to say, their explanation of the world -- of life and death -- of origin and destiny.

I concluded that all religions had substantially the same origin, and that in fact there has never been but one religion in the world. The twigs and leaves may differ, but the trunk is the same.

The poor African that pours out his heart to deity of stone is on an exact religious level with the robed priest who supplicates his God. The same mistake, the same superstition, bends the knees and shuts the eyes of both. Both ask for supernatural aid, and neither has the slightest thought of the absolute uniformity of nature.

It seems probable to me that the first organized ceremonial religion was the worship of the sun. The sun was the "Sky Father," the "All Seeing," the source of life -- the fireside of the world. The sun was regarded as a god who fought the darkness, the power of evil, the enemy of man.

There have been many sun-gods, and they seem to have been the chief deities in the ancient religions. They have been worshiped in many lands, by many nations that have passed to death and dust.

Apollo was a sun-god and he fought and conquered the serpent of night. Baldur was a sun-god. He was in love with the Dawn -- a maiden. Krishna was a sun-god. At his birth the Ganges was thrilled from its source to the sea, and all the trees, the dead as well as the living, burst into leaf and bud and flower. Hercules was a sun-god and so was Samson, whose strength was in his hair -- that is to say, in his beams. He was shorn of his strength by Delilah, the shadow -- the darkness. Osiris, Bacchus, and Mithra, Hermes, Buddha, and Quetzalcoatl, Prometheus, Zoroaster, and Perseus, Cadom, Lao-tsze, Fo-hi, Horus and Rameses, were all sun gods.

All of these gods had gods for fathers and their mothers were virgins. The births of nearly all were announced by stars, celebrated by celestial music, and voices declared that a blessing had come to the poor world. All of these gods were born in humble places -- in caves, under trees, in common inns, and tyrants sought to kill them all when they were babes. All of these sun-gods were born at the winter solstice -- on Christmas. Nearly all were worshiped by "wise men." All of them fasted for forty days -- all of them taught in parables -- all of them wrought miracles -- all met with a violent death, and all rose from the dead.

The history of these gods is the exact history of our Christ.

This is not a coincidence -- an accident. Christ was a sun-god. Christ was a new name for an old biography -- a survival -- the last of the sun-gods. Christ was not a man, but a myth -- not a life, but a legend.

I found that we had not only borrowed our Christ -- but that all our sacraments, symbols and ceremonies were legacies that we received from the buried past. There is nothing original in Christianity.

The cross was a symbol thousands of years before our era. It was a symbol of life, of immortality -- of the god Agni, and it was chiseled upon tombs many ages before a line of our Bible was written.

Baptism is far older than Christianity -- than Judaism. The Hindus, Egyptians, Greeks and Romans had Holy Water long before a Catholic lived. The Eucharist was borrowed from the Pagans. Ceres was the goddess of the fields -- Bacchus of the vine. At the harvest festival they made cakes of wheat and said: "This is the flesh of the goddess." They drank wine and cried: "This is the blood of our god."

The Egyptians had a Trinity. They worshiped Osiris, Isis and Horus, thousands of years before the Father, Son, and Holy Ghost were known.

The Tree of Life grew in India, in China, and among the Aztecs, long before the Garden of Eden was planted.

Long before our Bible was known, other nations had their sacred books.

The dogmas of the Fall of Man, the Atonement and Salvation by Faith, are far older than our religion.

In our blessed gospel, -- in our "divine scheme," -- there is nothing new -- nothing original. All old -- all borrowed, pieced and patched.

Then I concluded that all religions had been naturally produced, and that all were variation, modifications of one, -- then I felt that I knew that all were the work of man.

# Index

# C

# D

# E

heliocentric hypothesis 17-23
Heliopolis 36
herbalists 140, 147
Hercules 30, 31, 37-39, 150, 152, 178
Hermes 178
Herod, King 152
Hesus of the Druids 150, 154
Hill, J.H. IX, 15
Hinduism 26, 28, 132, 152, 154, 157, 166, 178
Hippocrates 141
Hislop, Alexander 173-174
Holocaust of WWII 129
Holy Ghost 47, 154
Holy War 127-129
homosexuality 137
Horus 75, 81, 117, 150-153, 155, 178, 180
Huxley, Thomas Henry 165
Hydra 39
Hypatia 91, 143

# I

Iesus 84, 95
Inca 122
India 61
indulgences 96, 133, 138
Ingersoll, Robert Green 177
Inquisition 132
Iraq 118
Isaiah 31
Isis 117, 152, 155, 180
Islam 90, 128
Israel 26

# J

Jackson, John G. 173, 175
Jacob 26
January 55
Janus 55
Jerusalem 37, 44, 127-128
Jesus IX, 84, 95, 149, 151, 154, 160, 161, 164, 167
Jesus Mysteries, the 174
Jews 4, 134-135, 140
Job 19, 32, 69
John 27, 29, 36, 48, 57, 62, 93
John the Baptist 54
Josephus 85
Judah 129
Judaism 4, 93, 127, 178
Judaizing 137
Judas 129
Judea 65, 75-76, 77, 84
Judgment Day 78
June 54
Juno 150
Jupiter 25, 28
Jupiter Pluvius 28

# K

Kings 47
King Solomon's Temple 128
Knights Templar, the 133-134
Koran 90
Krishna 75, 150-153, 156, 178

## L

Lakota 121
lamb 63, 155
Last Supper 49
Latin 50, 66, 69, 84, 96
Lazarus 58
Lent 42
Leo 23, 38, 56, 58, 60-61
Leviticus 130
Libra 23, 103
longest day of the year 23
Lord of Evil 29, 34, 35, 42, 59, 104
Lord of Good 29, 34, 35
Lord's Supper 49
Luke 47, 57
Lutheran Church 138-139
Luther, Martin 96-97, 138-140, 145-148

## M

Mack, Burton 175
magi 2, 42
March 45-47
Marduk 115-116
Mark 57, 93, 160
Mars 25, 26, 150
Martin Luther 138-140
Matthew 42, 49, 50, 55, 57, 77
Mayence 150
medical treatment 140
medieval inquisition 133-134
menstruation 140-141
Mercury 25
Metempsychosis 67
Michael 57

Michaelmas 50
Midgard Serpent, the 159
midwives 147
Mithra 151, 178
monotheism 28
months 54
moon 18, 25
Mortara, Edgardo 136
Moses 156
Muhammad 128
Muslims 15, 127, 134-135, 166
myrrh 42

## N

nativity 41
Nazarites 74
Nazi 139
Neo-Druids 154
nether world 18-19
New Testament 62, 86, 93-94, 98, 155, 157, 160
Nicaea 88
Nile 60, 64, 65, 73, 75, 83, 103, 151
Nimrod 39
Nimroud 39
Ninety-Five Theses, the 138-139
Nirvana 67-69
Noah IX, 21, 131, 137
Norse creation myth 120
Norse flood story 120
Nut 116-117

# O

Odin 120, 159
Ogdoad, the 117
Old Testament 4, 39, 93-94, 130
Onesimus 130
Oranos 118
Oriental philosophy 27
original sin 35, 141, 145
Orion 39
Osiris 116-117, 151, 158, 178, 180

# P

Pachacamac 122
Pagan Christ, the 98, 155, 171
Pagan Origins of the Christ Myth 173
Pan 26
parting of the Red Sea, the 156
Pascal, Blaise 80
Passion plays 44-45
Passion week 43-44
Passover 46
Pena, Francisco 124
Pentateuch 4
Perseus 46, 178
Peter 55, 69-70, 79
Philemon 130
Philo 85
Philolaus 18
Phlegethon 68
Phoenix 36
pillars of heaven 21
Pisces 23, 43, 61, 63, 77
plague 140
planets 22
Pliny 28, 81
Pluto 95

polytheism 28
Ponticus, Heraclides 18
Pontius Pilate 129
Pontus 73, 118
Pope Leo X 96
Portuguese Inquisition 135
Poseidon 118
primal fire 29
Prometheus 178
Prometheus Bound 44
Protestant Reformation 15, 101, 138-143
Ptah 117
Ptolemian Dynasty 73
Ptolemy Lagus 73
purgatory 69, 95-96
Puritans 141-143
Pythagoras 69, 150, 151
Pythais 150

# Q

Quakers 130
Quetzalcoatl 153, 178

# R

Ra 117
racism 130-131
radiometric age dating 126
ram 62
Ramseses 178
Raphael 57
redemption 34-35
Reformation 15, 101, 138-143
reincarnation 67
Religious Society of Friends 130
resurrection 34, 37, 45-46

# Other Books of Ancient Wisdom

## The Sweat Lodge is For Everyone

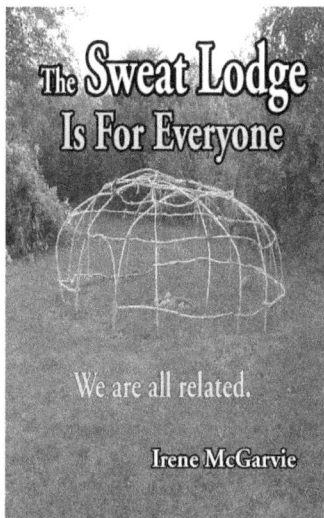

**ISBN 978-0-9737470-6-5  $19.95**

The Native American Sweat Lodge Ceremony offers so many benefits, both spiritual and physical for anyone who has the opportunity to take part in one.

This book is the non-Native's guide to understanding, participating in, and benefiting from Native American Sweat Lodge ceremonies.

## Messages in Your Tea Cup

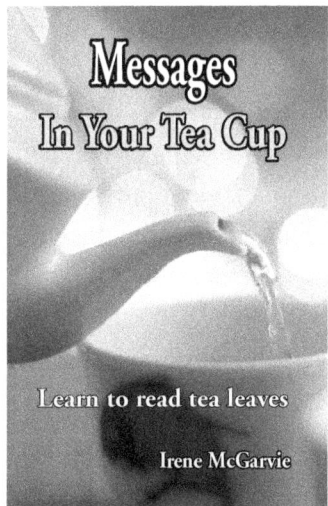

**ISBN 978-0-9783939-6-0  $19.95**

Have you ever wished that you could predict the future? Throughout history people all over the world have been able to predict future events and get advice from"beyond" through tea leaf reading.

This book will teach you everything that you need to know to begin reading tea leaves immediately.

# Other Books of Ancient Wisdom

## Séances in Washington

**Séances in Washington:**

Abraham Lincoln and Spiritualism during the Civil War

Nettie Colburn Maynard

**ISBN 978-0-9783939-7-7  $19.95**

Abraham Lincoln and Spiritualism during the Civil War.

This book is the first-hand account of the experiences of a Spiritualist medium in Washington during the Civil War. It created tremendous controversy when it was originally published in 1891, but there were enough credible witnesses to confirm her account of events that it could not be disputed.

## The Spirituality of Money

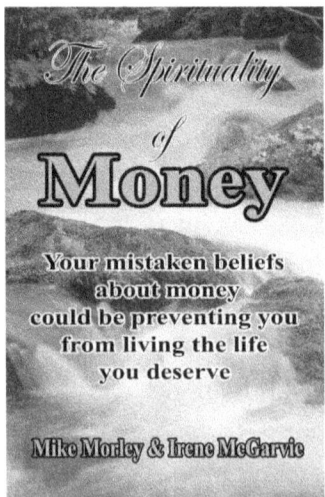

*The Spirituality of* **Money**

Your mistaken beliefs about money could be preventing you from living the life you deserve

Mike Morley & Irene McGarvie

**ISBN 978-0-9783939-3-9  $9.95**

Does it feel like money is a constant struggle for you? We keep hearing about how easy it is to "manifest" anything we want, including money, but for most people it just isn't that easy.

This book will help you recognize the false beliefs about money that are preventing you from living the life of affluence and abundance that you deserve.